# Language in a Changing Europe

*Papers from the*
*Annual Meeting of the British Association for Applied Linguistics*
*held at the University of Salford, September 1993*

Edited by

## David Graddol and Stephen Thomas

BRITISH ASSOCIATION FOR APPLIED LINGUISTICS
in association with
MULTILINGUAL MATTERS LTD
Clevedon • Philadelphia • Adelaide

**British Library Cataloguing in Publication Data**

A CIP catalogue record for this book is available from the British Library.

ISBN 1-85359-300-1 (pbk)

Published by the British Association for Applied Linguistics in association with Multilingual Matters Ltd.

**Multilingual Matters Ltd**
*UK*: Frankfurt Lodge, Clevedon Hall, Victoria Road, Clevedon, Avon BS21 7SJ.
*USA*: 1900 Frost Road, Suite 101, Bristol, PA 19007, USA.
*Australia*: P.O. Box 6025, 83 Gilles Street, Adelaide, SA 5000, Australia.

Printed and bound in Great Britain by the Longdunn Press, Bristol.

# Contents

# Preface

The twelve papers in this volume are selected from those presented at the 26th Annual Meeting of British Association for Applied Linguistics, held at the University of Salford, September 1993. When the organization for this conference began in 1991, the event which seemed to loom largest in most people's minds was the creation of a single market in Europe. After the 31st of December 1991 new legislation was to come into effect bringing about closer European integration and the so-called four freedoms – the free movement of people, goods, services and capital within Europe. The organizers felt that the theme of the annual conference should in some way reflect these new aspirations. We were, in other words, to stop contemplating our navels and become engaged with vital contemporary issues. What more important opportunity to plunge into the real world then than that presented by European integration and its affect on language? Thus arose the theme of *Language in a Changing Europe*.

Prof Ruth Wodak, a keynote speaker, warned against complacency and noted the dangers in not having a coherent policy towards racial and linguistic minorities. The picture of racism which immigrants faced in Austria was one to be taken seriously.

Many of the papers reflect BAAL's traditional concern with foreign language teaching, though often in the context of an integrated Europe. Bloor re-examines the Council of Europe syllabus, and concludes that despite the fact that the specifications for *Waystage* and *Threshold* levels have made an important contribution to language teaching in Europe, they have not always been applied with appropriate learner groups. Piper seeks to find ways in which the profession of Engineering might be given a more European dimension, and makes proposals for teaching foreign languages to non-specialist linguists.

Young's view of the obdurately monolingual nature of much of the British population is depressing within the context of a multilingual and multicultural Europe. The paper contrasts the negative attitudes towards foreign language teaching in Britain with those in France. Young concludes, perhaps noncontroversially, that French attitudes are far more positive and that the French sociolinguistic environment is more supportive than its British counterpart.

Although Young's paper presents us with a gloomy picture of monolingual 'little Englanders', Huang and Milroy redress this picture to some extent by reminding us that Britain is in fact rich in linguistic diversity. Their study examines the language preference and code switching of the Tyneside Chinese community, and argues that these phenomena should be viewed from a wider sociolinguistic perspective.

Steel and Anderson have made a preliminary investigation of the psycholinguistic abilities of first year undergraduate French learners and have produced some perhaps surprising findings regarding the correlation of metalinguistic knowledge with proficiency in French. Hughes et al have produced a work in progress report, which represents an important move to rehabilitate the teaching of grammar in the EFL classroom. They discuss the pedagogic benefits of looking at grammar from the point of view of contexts beyond the sentence, with grammar seen as a set of skills and not as a mere body of knowledge.

Cutting discusses an application for EAP students of the formation of a discourse community. The community in this instance is that of the students' common room for the MSc. in Applied Linguistics at the University of Edinburgh. Lea considers the difficulties faced by students with non traditional educational backgrounds in academic writing, in the context of the various influences on students' writing practices.

Parkinson and Davies discuss a project which is intended to function within research and teacher development. The project is concerned with ways of providing teachers with opportunities to observe each other and examines the relevance of a coding system which might be used for this purpose.

Moving away from the specific concerns of language teaching Kelly presents a model of inter-cultural advertising in the German Democratic Republic. Kelly makes the important point that despite sharing a linguistic code East and West Germany remain different in culture. This theme of communicative conflict within the 'new Germany' is developed by Stevenson. Through an analysis of forms of public discourse Stevenson concludes that the East/West dichotomy continues as a problem of intercultural communication. In effect, the removal of the formal barriers between speech communities has not led to the expected change in cultural practices. A fact which the European politicians should not ignore.

In the moments when members of the conference were able to talk informally, the theme of the conference was often reflected in a desire to protest against some of the more reactionary movements in language policy which have recently emerged in Britain. The need was frequently expressed that we should strive to be a part of Europe and indeed the rest of the world: to be concerned with its language policies and attitudes towards minority language groups, and to make our voices and expertise felt. These were all aspects of the theme which we had hoped would be provoked and aired, and it is because such views were voiced that we feel optimistic, though not complacent, about the future of *Language in a Changing Europe*.

*Stephen Thomas*

# 1 The Development and Forms of Racist Discourse in Austria since 1989

RUTH WODAK
*University of Vienna*

## Introduction

In contrast to the United States, where Applied Linguistics is mainly concerned with the issues of language teaching and language learning, Applied Linguistics in continental Europe has always comprised discourse analysis as well: communication in institutions, media discourse, political discourse, discourse and gender, as well as racist discourse. The notion 'applied' is significant because studies in the domains mentioned above frequently attempt to provide guidelines to 'apply', for example, how doctors could be trained to communicate differently and more effectively with patients, or how in our case, multicultural curricula are to be created and implemented, new textbooks for foreign language teaching have to be written, new methods of language teaching have to be adapted etc. (eg Wodak, Menz and Lalouschek, 1989).

It is in this much broader tradition of Applied Linguistics and specifically in the study of the discourses of racism and prejudices that I would like to place my paper. Thus, I would like to discuss some discursive forms of racist talk, taking the Austrian case as my point of departure and as the source of my examples. My aims are threefold: First, to say a bit about the general theory and methodology of discourse analysis in relationship to the study of prejudice and racism. Second, I wish to explain the discourse-historical approach in discourse analysis. This methodological approach, which we developed in the course of a two-year study of post-war antisemitism in Austria, attempts to analyze discourses by attending to their historical, socio-political and setting-specific contexts (Wodak et al., 1990; Wodak, 1991a, 1991b). This type of analysis is of particular relevance when analyzing allusions and ambiguous formulations in texts, where the interpretation proves to be crucially dependent on this wider context. Third, I would like to illustrate the usefulness of the discourse-historical approach by offering examples taken from the Austrian print and

1

Graddol, D and Thomas, S. (1994)
*Language in a Changing Europe,*
Clevedon: BAAL and Multilingual Matters

electronic media dealing with foreigners immediately after the collapse of the ruling regimes in eastern Europe (eg Mitten and Wodak, 1993; Wodak and Matouschek,1993). Specifically, I would like to focus on the development of racist discourse by examining the 'discourse history' chronologically, to show 'racism *in statu nascendi*'.

In pursuing these aims, I will also need to discuss some important historical facts about Austria. In my view, Austrian historical specificities distinguish the contents and to some extent, the forms of racist discourse in Austria from discourses with similar functions in other countries. To cite but one example, in general Hungarians and Czechs are viewed more positively in Austria than are Rumanians and Poles. This is traceable to some extent to perceived cultural affinities with these former groups dating from the time of the Austro-Hungarian empire, and to some extent to a kind of residual historical memory in Austria of Hungarians and Czechs as once heroic fighters against Soviet tanks. At the same time, and somewhat anomalously, the fall of the 'iron curtain' and the accompanying end of the cold war marked a major caesura in attitudes inside Austria towards potential immigrants from eastern Europe, transforming former heroic escapees from Communist tyranny into contemporary 'criminal tourists'. Media images – and this is the main point I would like to address today – have been instrumental in constructing and reinforcing the prejudiced terms of the debate on the so-called 'foreigner problem'.

It is essential in this connection to reiterate the significance and influence of the choice of topics by social elites such as politicians, journalists, etc on the formation of prejudice among the broader political public. As Teun Van Dijk writes, summarizing his many years of research on prejudiced discourse:

> most ethnic news stories are not reproductions of the conversational stories. On the contrary, everyday stories often ˜eproduce media stories. It is in this sense (only) that the media (claim to) provide what the public 'wants'... Against this background, we have reasons, and empirical evidence, to assume that elite groups provide the initial (pre)formulations of ethnic prejudices in society, and that the media are the major channel and the communicative context for such discourse. (Van Dijk 1989: 361)

## Some Facts about Austria

The Austrian First Republic was established in 1918. Since 1945, Austria has undergone many political and sociological changes. It was occupied by Allied forces for ten years after the war and became an independent and neutral country in 1955, though its political institutions owed more to western than to eastern European influence. An 'economic miracle' was accompanied by the creation of an advanced welfare state on the Swedish model. In 1956, during the anti-Stalinist uprising, 160,000

Hungarians entered Austria, most on their way elsewhere, and were heartily welcomed, though the economic situation in Austria was not particularly favourable. In 1968, almost 100,000 Czechs came to Austria after the crushing of the 'Prague Spring', and again there were no complaints. In the early 1980s, almost 50,000 Poles fled to Austria after the declaration of martial law, and these, too, were greeted with varying degrees of enthusiasm. The big change occurred in 1989 and 90, when the 'iron curtain' fell and thousands of citizens from former Warsaw Pact countries travelled to Austria.

Today, Austria has become a multicultural society, although many would not like to hear such a statement. Austria contains several different types of foreigners and minorities: autochthonous minorities (Slovenes, Croats, Hungarians, Jews, Gypsies, Czechs and Slovaks); immigrant workers (mainly Turks and Yugoslavs who began arriving in the 1970s); political refugees of all stripes (including Iranians, Vietnamese, Hungarians, Czechs, Poles, Albanians, Bosnians etc.); and, since 1989, the new so-called 'economic refugees', (predominantly Hungarians, Poles, Czechs, Rumanians and Russians). Each of these categories has a different legal status: some non-native citizens of other countries have become naturalized citizens; some have acquired refugee status; others are permanent or temporary residents. (see Bauböck et al., 1991, Fassmann and Münz, 1992).

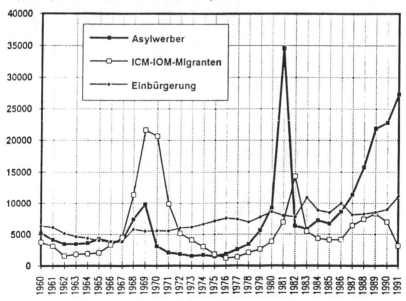

*Figure 1 Austria as country of asylum 1960-1991*

By 1991, approximately 400,000 foreigners lived in Austria, around 5.3% of the total population. This corresponds roughly to the percentage of foreign workers and their family members who lived in Austria in the 1970s. Thus, when comparing percentages, nothing much has changed in the last twenty years. Yet the perception of change is pervasive, as is constantly implied by the reporting of the press about the hugh masses of immigrants having entered recently or about to enter.

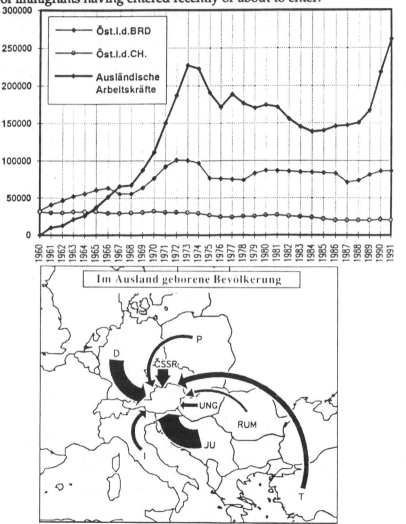

*Figure 2 (top) Foreign employees in Austria 1960-1991*
*Figure 3 (bottom) Origin of foreigners*

# Neo-Racism in Contemporary Austria: A discourse-historical study

In 1991, the Department of Applied Linguistics at the University of Vienna began a pilot study entitled 'Austria's Attitudes towards Its East-Central European Neighbours. Studies on Xenophobic Public Discourse'. The aim of the study was to discern the attitudes Austrians had towards Hungarians, Czechs and Slovaks, Poles and Rumanians in the years 1988-1990 and to investigate in what ways they had altered both historically as well as more recently. Specifically, the study examined – both quantitatively and qualitatively – neo-racist utterances (as opposed to 'classical fascist and nationalsocialist racism during the Nazi period) and discursive strategies in regional and national newspapers, weekly news magazines (2000 articles), and television and radio news and features broadcasts (20 hours video). In addition, interviews were conducted with politicians and with randomly selected respondents. As in an earlier study on post-war antisemitism (Wodak, et al. 1990), sociolinguistic, psycholinguistic and text linguistic approaches were applied in a 'discourse-historical' way: original sources, the precise social and political contexts and social psychological factors were integrated into the analysis.

Space does not permit a lengthy digression on the various concepts of racism and prejudice, but I would like to provide a working definition of the concept 'prejudice', which I have borrowed from Teun van Dijk. According to van Dijk,

> 'Prejudice', is both a cognitive and a social phenomenon. It is not merely a characteristic of individual beliefs or emotions about social groups, but a shared form of social representation in group members, acquired during social processes of socialisation and transformed and enacted in social communication and interaction. (van Dijk 1989, 13)

In my view, though prejudice is constituted and becomes manifest through, and is transported by language, there is no specific 'language of prejudice', but rather prejudiced language use, which varies according to the context in which it occurs. The discourse-historical approach concentrates on three dimensions of prejudiced language use: the content of prejudiced remarks (which vary according to the targeted social group); argumentation strategies (i.e. cohesive devices in texts which serve specific argumentative aims); and linguistic forms of realization (generalizations, stories, etc.). I will illustrate each of these three dimensions below.

## The Development of Topics in the Media as an Indicator of Change in Attitudes towards Austria's East Central European Neighbours

In general, communication about minorities is centred thematically around a few elements such as *difference, deviance,* and *perceived threat.* According to a frequently occuring generalization, foreigners damage the host country's socio-economic interests. The emphasis here is on the threat to economic interests due to competition, particularly the unfair competition offered by the shadow labour market. Another such generalization holds that 'they' (i.e. foreigners) are also different in terms of culture, mentality, etc. Here, the emphasis is on the perceived threat to the dominant cultural order. Foreigners are also said to be involved in activities that are viewed negatively (e.g. loudness) or are said to be criminally inclined. The emphasis in this latter prejudice is on the threat deviance poses to the established social order.

In our study tracing the development of public discourse in Austria on the so-called new 'foreigner and refugee problem', we found a strong temporal correlation between the new freedom of travel and emigration in the former 'iron curtain' countries and the evident change of attitude towards our Eastern neighbours. With the first great wave of travellers beginning in 1988 came a major increase in the applications for political asylum. The 'refugee problem' and the fears accompanying it thus became one of the most important issues of public life in Austria (and elsewhere).

The public discussion about foreigners, beginning in 1989, initially yielded a *discourse of sympathy* for those freeing themselves from the Communist yoke. This discourse then developed into what I have termed a *discourse of tutelage,* and in the end evolved into an aggressive *discourse of defensive self-justification.* Throughout, however, the content of many of the prejudices remained constant, but were employed and re-deployed to accommodate the discursive demands of an altered political situation. The range of linguistic realizations (our third dimension) is very broad; it reaches from allusions and insinuations to blatant and crudely racist statements. The new residency law, and the widespread assent it has met, may indeed be seen as a culmination of sorts, but this assent could build upon a specific history and evolution of discursive practices about the 'foreigner problem'.

The absurd lengths to which this discourse led may be illustrated by an unintentionally humorous aspect of party electoral propaganda. During the campaign prior to the 1990 elections to the Austrian National Assembly, public discourse in the print media and by several leading politicians became fully dominated by the subject of foreigners. Playing on the increasing hostility towards foreigners, the Vienna chapter of the Freedom Party of Austria, a party sharing many features with Le Pen in France, put up a campaign poster declaring 'Vienna must not allowed to become Chicago!'. This slogan apparently had the intended effect, for the FPÖ was able to more than double its previous number of votes. (Plasser and Ulram 1991a). But what does this bewildering slogan mean?

At first glance, it does seem to evoke associations with criminality identified in the popular imagination with large American cities in general, and, because Chicago was chosen, possibly alludes to filmic and television depictions of Al Capone and his ilk. However, one fact about Chicago does suggest another element of meaning this poster might have been designed to elicit, namely, that Chicago is the city with the largest concentration of people of Polish heritage outside Poland. If this pattern were related discursively, as it was temporally, to the dominant campaign issue of 'foreign criminality', there seems to be little doubt that the Freedom Party slogan about Chicago was a characteristically allusive formula designed to trigger just the kind of xenophobic resentment the new wave of 'criminal tourism' had unleashed.

In an opinion poll published in 1991, 84% percent of those questioned reported having had no negative experiences with foreigners in the months prior to the poll, 69% had had no contact with foreigners in their neighbourhoods, and 70% counted no foreigners among their friends or acquaintances. Yet it was precisely among respondents with the least direct contact with foreigners that fear and hatred of foreigners were the most pronounced. This dissonance between personal experience and negative attitude is known to be the most fertile territory for the formation and reproduction of neo-racist prejudice against ethnic minorities.

Of course, political leaders on the right do their best to promote such images. Jörg Haider, the leader of the Freedom Party, the party with the aversion to Chicago, in 1992 addressed a group of police officers on the topic of 'security', in the district in Vienna which has the highest concentration of foreigners:

> Here at home we have, you might say, the South American mafia, which has specialized in pick-pocketing and at their own training camps in Italy received the introductory course from the Mafia before they were released to Austria. We have Poles who have organized themselves and concentrated on auto theft. We have citizens of former Yugoslavia who are experts in breaking into private homes, and if you should ever lose your house keys, call on them to get back into your houses really fast. We have Turks who have set up excellent organizations in the field of Heroin and we have Russians, who today are proven experts in the area of extortion and of muggings.

# Argumentation Strategies in Prejudiced Discourse

I would like to turn to our second dimension of analysis, strategies of argumentation. If we except the kind of open appeals to racism characteristic of Haider, we see that such strategies involve the linking of discrete but related contents in a given text which convey prejudice (in the present context, neo-racist prejudice) while simultaneously seeking to disguise it. (Wodak et al., 1990; Wodak, 1991a) Of the many such strategies available, I would like to mention two.

The first are *strategies of group definition and construction*, strategies which assist in constituting a 'we discourse'. The linguistic forms of realizing this constitution of an ingroup and outgroup (our third dimension) include

(a)    the use of grammatically cohesive elements (personal pronouns, depersonalization [*Anonymisierung*], generalization and equation of incommensurable phenomena [*Gleichsetzung*];

(b)    the use of vague characterizations;

(c)    the substantive definition of groups.

An essential function of 'we discourse' is the denial of personal responsibility and its displacement onto the group as a whole, in the sense that what many people believe cannot be wrong.

In a similar vein, *strategies of self-justification* enable speakers to make normative evaluations of the outgroup and to assign guilt or responsibility to members of that group or to the group as a whole. The aim of such a discourse of self-justification, which is closely wound up with 'we discourse', is to allow the speaker to present herself or himself as free of prejudice or even as a victim of so-called 'reverse' prejudice.

# The Development of a Public Racist Discourse: Media discourse about Rumania and Rumanians

To illustrate these strategies, I would like to turn to media discourse proper about Rumania and Rumanians, I should start by stating the obvious. In public situations where anonymity is assured, speakers exhibit little or no inhibitions in expressing their prejudices.

As our analytical focus moves away from such discursive situations into settings and contexts of increasing personal exposure, however, we are confronted with a much more complex array of strategic discursive features employed to express the same or similar prejudices. This is, in our view, traceable to an increasing intrusion into a speaker's consciousness of the normative expectations associated with these various public settings.

The most significant example concerns the development of forms of racist discourse I mentioned above: the discourses of sympathy, of tutelage and of defensive self-justification. As I suggested above, the point of departure of every form of prejudiced discourse is the constitution of groups. The recent events in the former Warsaw Pact countries led to an increasing media presence of Poles, Hungarians, Czechs, Slovaks and Rumanians, but, and this was the most important development, presented as members of their respective national communities rather than ethnically interchangeable victims of Communism.

The reporting on the fall of Ceaucescu at Christmas time in 1989 represented an initial climax of public discourse about Rumanians. The stories in the media focussed on poverty, illness, and violence as well as on the assistance that had been collected and shipped by the Austrian population. This, in other words, is what we have described as a discourse of sympathy.

After the initial phase of revolutionary events had run their course, politicians and so-called experts alike began to discuss more openly what should be done for and with these countries. The situation in Rumania was estimated and evaluated by Austrian experts, and proposals were advanced in Austria on how best to inaugurate a 'real' democracy, but the opinions of those potentially affected by these decisions in Rumania were seldom sought.

This is what we have described as a discourse of tutelage. Chronologically, the third stage of the development towards a new quality of discourse was the period in which the population took notice of the fact that even after the 'liberation', Rumanians were still coming to Austria seeking asylum. At this point, sympathy for the Rumanians all but dissipated. They were no longer patronized as naive or immature; rather, in the print media and in public discourse the Rumanians began to be disparaged. This distant foreign group thus soon became the outgroup par excellence, inside Austria. From approximately the beginning of May 1990, then, it is possible to detect in public discourse increasingly hostile prejudiced attitudes and expressions towards Rumanians, most of which appear in the form of what we have termed the discourses of defensive self-justification.

To illustrate these developments I would first like to present a few excerpts from that most public of media, the television news broadcasts of the Austrian national broadcasting company (ORF). The ORF is similar to the BBC in that it is a state-supported and viewer-funded institution that has a statutory commitment to 'objectivity' in the transmission of news. But, unlike the BBC, it has a monopoly on broadcasting in Austria (apart from cable) and Austrian television does run commercials, though not during programs.

In the following, the first example of the discourse of sympathy is taken from a commentary on the news by Paul Lendvai, the ORF in-house expert on Eastern European affairs, on 22 December 1989. Lendvai's comments typify the presentation of the foreign group as a humiliated, exploited, impoverished people. At one point Lendvai stated:

> The long pent-up anger of a people who had been deprived of their rights, muzzled, spied upon and humiliated daily, has put paid to all predictions, to all cliches. In the common European house now emerging, Ceaucescu's Rumania was a torture chamber in the truest sense of the word.

The second example contains two parts: a sound bite from the Austrian Chancellor Franz Vranitzky from 22 December 1989, and the text of the news itself two days later. Both illustrate the positive self-presentation of the ingroup, especially its sympathy and willingness to help. Vranitzky was shown on the news stating that:

> it is certainly a very terrible thing that we (sic!) are very probably going to have violence and dead and injured.

On the news on 24 December, 1989, the news reader stated, quite in the spirit of Christmas eve, that:

> Austria is helping the Rumanian people. All sorts of aid are unreservedly being brought to collection points.... Therefore please, do not give up donating, keep on proving your generous readiness to help.

The third example, taken from the Lower Austrian local television news broadcast from 10 January 1990, assigns guilt for all ills and evils to a scapegoat, in this case the Ceaucescu regime. The news reader stated:

> [In] Transylvania, Dracula's homeland, Ceaucescu and his wife systematically sucked the blood out of the country.... Elena Ceaucescu is being represented as a modern zombie... The hatred of this dictator family, [as well as] Ceaucescu's madness are omnipresent. Even in villages which are still partly idyllic.

What strikes one about this final example is the use of the allusion to Dracula ('evocation'/ switch to another genre) to ascribe sanguinary lust to Ceausescu, from which followed the Rumanians' thirst for vengeance. The motifs of hatred and revenge are continuously emphasized in the reporting; at the same time, understanding for these feelings on the part of Austrians (or at least on the part of the Austrian news reader) is indicated by the description of the Rumanians' miserable living conditions. This alleged motif of thirst for revenge, for which there was actually very little empirical evidence (for example, in the sense of spontaneous explosions of mass terror or lynch mobs), became a set piece in the reporting on Rumania, and was an important preparatory stage leading to the emergence of what we have termed the discourse of tutelage.

The successor discourse in our history of discursive practices to the discourse of sympathy, the discourse of tutelage, emphasized the (presumed) competence of Austrians in questions of democracy, while at the same time belittling the Rumanians' own. If one examines the reports chronologically, there are, of course, numerous overlappings; however, the discourse of sympathy and helpfulness increasingly gave way to the discourse of tutelage.

In this discourse, the foreign group as a whole as well as individuals in it are presented as immature, naive, backward in questions of democracy, and either not at all, or not yet, suitable to the task of constructing a democratic community. The Austrians, who can 'tutor' the foreigners in proper civic behaviour, are portrayed as exhibiting democratic maturity and, more importantly, expert knowledge of the possibilities for democracy in Rumania.

These sentiments are realized linguistically principally in the form of contrived oppositions of good and bad and through discourse representation. Discourse representation can take the form of direct quotations as well as the German subjunctive for indirect speech. Often, however, it takes the form of presenting the views of presumed Austrian political experts while neglecting those of Rumanians experiencing these upheavals, or of Rumanian political experts.

For example, the evening television news on 22 December 1989 contained an interview with former Austrian Chancellor Bruno Kreisky. The news reader asked Kreisky, 'What would your personal advice to the population be at this moment in time?... Do you think that the situation in the east is already stable enough that democracy could take root?' to which Kreisky replied, 'I think that there can be democracy there in the long term. But I wouldn't like to say that we are already over the mountain'. On the same programme, the ORF's own expert, Lendvai, was called upon for his views. To the news reader's question, 'Professor Lendvai, back to Manescu, the new man. Do you think he is capable of leading his country into a better future?' Lendvai answered:

> Not at all.... I met him in 1964 when he was foreign minister. He was, in fact, a very affable fellow, but he was a political light weight. [An] extraordinarily handsome man, and the talk of the town in Bucharest was always to which reception would he be going with which girlfriend.... He speaks excellent French.... but he could play a certain role as a symbol, as a figurehead, let us say, for the transition period.

If the reports in the electronic and print media treated the revolutionary events in Rumania between December 1989 and February 1990 as foreign events, transmitting the images and messages outlined

above, the character and (prejudiced) quality of reporting changed
notably once increasing numbers of Rumanians began making their way
towards Austria. Rumanians were no longer greeted with sympathy,
but rather with open rejection. From around the 1st of March 1990,
Rumanians were perceived as representing a new threat (however
conceived) to the Austrians. The break in the discourse pattern came,
when the media and thus the public became aware of the Interior
Ministry's plan to house 800 young male Rumanians seeking political
asylum in an unused barracks located in Kaisersteinbruch, a small
village of 200 inhabitants.

Emblematic of the prejudices identified with this new discursive
'turn' are the following passages taken from an article which appeared
in Austria's leading tabloid, the *Neue Kronenzeitung*. I will analyze this
article along our three dimensions: The central theme of this article was
the fear of Kaisersteinbruch residents that their women would be raped
by the young Rumanian men, although at the time of the article there
was not a single Rumanian male in the village. Particularly striking are
the ways the author's own opinion intrudes into the ostensible news
article, either explicitly or by means of extremely vague discourse
representation. The interspersing of direct quotations and indirect
speech with the normal narrative indicative acts to transform the
individual fears of some into a generalized panic among the entire
village population, as the final sentence makes clear. The substantive
content of the prejudice 'the potential readiness of the Rumanians to
rape' is transmitted by means of a quote from an old village woman,
who alludes to the relations between the local population and the
Russian troops who occupied Austria from 1945-1955. The groundwork
for drawing the analogy between the Russians then and the Rumanians
now, however, is in fact laid by the author in the introductory section on
the historical 'origins of fear':

> ... an old woman from the village, who will not forget that time for as long
> as she lives, recalled. 'Yeah, do you think it things were done delicately
> back then? It was difficult for us women, alone, the men were away
> fighting, you know, or had been killed [in the war]. We knew [then] what
> it meant to be a sacrificial lamb. I can certainly understand that young
> women, who were only children back then, are afraid. Their husbands
> often work the night shift, and during the day there are only women
> around in the village. And now someone wants to bring in 800
> robust,strong, young, immature men?'

The analogy between the past and present, in the form of an allusion,
is unmistakable. The Russians, who were occupying the village, were
not 'delicate'. The men were not there, the women became (sexual)
sacrificial lambs. That the allusion is to sexual harassment or rape
ostensibly experienced by the village women at the hands of the

Russians, and not to non-sexual acts of violence, may be inferred from the adjectives used to describe the young Rumanians. These latter were not described as violent, aggressive, etc., but rather as young, strong (stronger than women), robust (possibly positively connoted in the sense of well-developed?) but especially as immature (emotionally immature in the intended sense). Actual rapists, most of whom were presumably young Russian soldiers at the end of the Second World War, are equated with immature Rumanian potential rapists. The comparison of the Russians, an occupying power in 1945 with these 800 Rumanians, all of whom were seeking assistance and political asylum, represents an additional and especially crude distortion.

However, the fears, anxieties and cries for help of the women in the village, which the main headline, the lead and the text of the article help to generalize through the use of vague discourse representation, are in fact only legitimated in the final paragraph of the article, with the quote from the woman villager. Conveying this and similar specific substantive contents, especially in the form of discourse representations, are among the most favoured linguistic means of transmitting prejudiced attitudes in the reporting of the *Neue Kronenzeitung*.

The attributes of laziness and disloyalty, which often appear in these contexts, refer principally to the belief that the Rumanians who come to Austria should remain in and help rebuild their own country. The reference itself – as the historical analysis implies – alludes to the official Austrian ideology that after the Second World War, the Austrians stayed put and rebuilt their country from the ruins. The substantial aid which Austria received from abroad after 1945 (i.e. the Marshall Plan) is usually left out of the account, and other relevant facts are also frequently denied or distorted. Thus, those Rumanians who come to Austria are believed to be taking flight for base motives, an attitude which received its linguistic christening as the dichotomy between genuine and 'economic' refugees. A not infrequent ancillary insinuation associated with the idea of Rumanians fleeing their country is that they are doing so to escape a criminal past at home (the bad ones come, the good ones stay at home).

Let us summarize the strategies of justification employed in prejudiced discourse about Rumanians which developed in 1989 and 1990. It served to defend the positive image of Austria as a 'traditional country of asylum' and the ostensible tolerant and humanitarian attitude of the Austrians. At the same time, this positive self-presentation served to justify the refusal to accept these Rumanian refugees, for though Austria is a traditional country of asylum, it is not a country to which 'economic refugees' might immigrate.

# Perspectives

Whenever we speak about others, we at the same time also determine who we are. It follows that discourses about others, about foreign or hostile groups, are at the same time also reflections of our own self-image. If this is so, then the really interesting question becomes, just who are the genuine Austrians, anyway? Are they everything that the others are perceived not to be? If there are Austrians on one side and Jews, foreigners, refugees, Slovenes, Turks, now and then a Yugoslav building superintendent, etc., then Austrians cannot be these. Many Austrians see themselves in this way, threatened with cultural extinction by the encroaching foreigners. The image of danger which out-groups represent and the emphasis on the Austrians as victims are tropes which recur incessantly in discourse about refugees or immigrants.

As an expression of collective self-recognition, the role of victim seems to draw on the consensus history of the emergence of the Second Austrian Republic. (Wodak et al. 1994; Mitten 1993). First, victim of National Socialism, then a victim of a Jewish conspiracy during the Waldheim affair, and more recently a victim of a changing political world at the end of the 1980s. Perhaps even the final victim of Communism, which now, *ex post facto*, unloads on the Austrians what it itself created: the 'masses' fleeing the poverty and destitution of the East.

Many Austrians do not realize or do not want to realize that the society has changed into a multicultural society. New problems have to be solved: how to create new curricula, how to write new textbooks and revise the old ones, how to combat the deep prejudices, and how to create and use a non-discriminatory language and discourse.

Quite on the contrary, Austria, today, seems to be torn by the extreme tension between its own ambivalent nationalism and its fear of becoming lost in a new unified Europe. Austrians, moreover, are trapped in a dilemma of searching for their own identity while trying to cope with their own history. At the same time, Austria is exposed to radical new developments through the migration from the East and through new tendencies which the end of the Cold War and the recent emergence of new structures in eastern Europe have thrown up.

Fights about language always manifest other, deeper sociological and political problems. Which is why we should try to understand them and cope with them explicitly. Mario Erdheim once described the tensions I alluded to above in a particularly apposite way. Erdheim wrote:

... Freud posits... a contrast... between aggression and culture. For him, culture, which increasingly binds people together, became a creation of Eros, while aggression isolates people from one another. From this perspective, hostility towards foreigners appears as a tendency which threatens culture as a whole. Violence against foreigners becomes a symptom which signifies the exhaustion of the culture's potential to change. This symptom is to be taken seriously, and one must investigate the preconditions for its emergence.

It would seem to follow that, whatever specificities it might exhibit, the problem of hostility towards foreigners in Austria is merely a kind of colloquial inflection of a far more embracing language of fear and aggression. In this sense, Austria's relations with those foreign to it is paradigmatic for its own self-understanding, for better or for worse. This enjoins us to continue to observe, to listen to, and to combat, Austria's particular historically conditioned *vernacular of exclusion*.

# References

Fassmann, H. and Münz, R. (1992) Einwanderungsland Österreich? *Gastarbeiter – Flüchtlinge – Immigranten.* (Hg. v.d. Österr. Akademie der Wissenschaften.) Wien.
Mitten, R. (1993) Die 'Judenfrage' im Nachkriegsösterreich. *Zeitgeschichte* 1/3.
Mitten R. and Wodak, R. (1993) On the Discourse of and Prejudice. In *Folia Linguistica*, Wien.
Plasser, F. and Ulram, P.A. (1991) *Ausländerfeindlichkeit als Wahlmotiv, Daten und Trends.* (Unpublished MS). Wien.
Van Dijk, T.A. (1989) *Communicating Racism.* Newbury Park: Sage.
Wodak, R. , Menz, F. and Lalouschek, J. (1989) *Sprachbarrieren.* Vienna: Edition Atelier.
Wodak, R. et al. (1990) '*Wir sind alle unschuldige Täter!' Diskurshistorische Studien zum Nachkriegsantisemitismus.* Frankfurt a.Main: Suhrkamp.
Wodak, R. (1991a) Turning the Tables: antisemitic Discourse in Postwar Austria. *Discourse and Society* 2/1, 1993.
Wodak, R. (1991b) *The Waldheim Phenomenon in Austria. Patterns of Prejudice.*
Wodak, R. and Matouschek, B. (1993) 'We are dealing with people whose origins one can clearly tell just by looking': critical discourse analysis and the study of neo-racism in contemporary Austria. In *Discourse and Society* 2 (4), 225-48
Wodak, R. et al., (1994) *Die Sprachen der Vergangenheiten. Öffentliches Gedenken in österreichischen und deutschen Medien.* Frankfurt a. Main: Suhrkamp.

# 2 Council of Europe Syllabus Revisited: Lessons for the future?

MERIEL BLOOR
*University of Warwick*

## Introduction

An essential factor in European unity is effective communication, and effective communication is dependant on excellent language teaching and learning. This was recognised as long ago as 1954 when the European Cultural Convention committed member states of the Council of Europe to improved provision for languages in education. The present paper re-considers the Council of Europe's contributions to language teaching, and in particular, the *Threshold Level* and *Waystage* Level in a Unit-Credit System. Essentially, I am claiming here that the Unit Credit System (usually known as 'The Council of Europe Syllabus'), although influential, has been under-used in the ways which were originally intended but over-used with learners for whom it is inappropriate. Above all, its use has been under-researched. This is not to attribute any blame to the original designers of the project, but it is worth noting that twenty years after the conception of the work, we are unable to properly evaluate the outcomes.

The Unit-Credit System was established in the first half of the 1970s, thanks primarily to the work of Van Ek, Alexander and Trim, and was revised in 1990 (Van Ek and Trim, 1992). At each stage, the work has been sponsored by the Council for Cultural Co-operation.

In 1992, in his AILA Review article, Trim claims that it is one of the major recent innovations in language teaching. However, apart from comments of this kind and word of mouth evidence, it is very difficult to establish the exact extent of its use and even more difficult to evaluate its success.

## The nature of the Unit-Credit System

The Council of Europe Syllabus is not, in fact, a *teaching* syllabus in the proper sense of the term and it was never claimed to be such by its authors. It is, rather, an attempt to outline the components of 'how a

16

Graddol, D and Thomas, S. (1994)
*Language in a Changing Europe,*
Clevedon: BAAL and Multilingual Matters

learner should be able to use a language in order to act independently in a country in which that language is the vehicle of communication in everyday life', or what in ESP terminology is known as a 'target needs specification'. This specification is presented in the original edition as being 'a set of operational objectives', which will 'suit the needs of the average man (*sic*) – and which is 'suitable as a basis for the establishment of a system of equivalences' for the learning of different European languages (Trim, 1975, *Introduction to the Threshold Level*).

In the 1990 edition, the authors refer to *The Threshold Level* as a document that 'has been used by designers of syllabuses' and this is as it should be. An adequate *teaching syllabus* has to be designed in relation to the starting level of the learners, their expectations, number of study hours and resources available, as well as providing a reasonable balance between different elements of the course.

The original specifications aimed to identify the language (in terms of the linguistic exponents of the *settings, functions*, and *notions*) that it would be necessary for a person to master in order to communicate reasonably successfully in the country of use. This was termed the 'Threshold Level' and thought to require approximately 400 hours of study. When course designers found the sheer size of the syllabus difficult to manage, a refined, shorter specification was devised called 'Waystage'.

The specifications were not originally drawn up for learners with specific needs (for example, for business or academic purposes). Van Ek (1992), however, claims that, although *Threshold Level* 1990 does not cater specifically for professional people, it is 'relevant' to their needs, – although this is debatable.

## The implementation of the system

According to Trim (1992), since 1975 the specifications have been made available in 12 European languages and have been used extensively across Europe as the basis for course design, curricular guidelines and exam syllabuses. The different language versions are not exact translations of each other (how could they be?), but are near equivalents in terms of what they set out to do.

But as I mentioned above, to the best of my knowledge, there has been very little external research into the use of the specifications. It is never easy to measure the extent (or evaluate the quality of) courses for adult language learners. Unlike school systems, where records are kept and formal exams are taken, adult language learning tends to be sporadic, unrecorded and often untested.

In Britain, at least, the influence of the 1975 publications has not been overt, and most Local Authority provision, in Colleges of Further

Education, for example, has missed the opportunity to establish courses based on the specifications. If one wished to attend an evening class in a European language, it is unlikely that one would find (or could ever have found) a course claiming to teach *Waystage* or *Threshold Level*. And yet there is little doubt that the original designers had in mind that all over Europe, institutions would provide courses of this type in the main European languages, leading to some type of common recognised certification. From the point of view of evaluation, this would be a highly desirable state of affairs, as certified courses that matched a common European standard would be valuable for language learners and for employers alike.

Such a system, if it were actually operating, would provide a basis for course and materials evaluation and for the objective comparison of teaching or self-study methods in different countries. It would also become possible to establish the average number of hours required to complete a course leading to the specifications since the guidelines in the latest publications are still vague and questionable.

Unfortunately, in Britain at least, the opportunity for using the specifications in state further education has now been lost with the introduction of the new languages Lead Body Standards linked to the National Vocational Qualifications. This new set of specifications, by the way, which at first sight appears to be a far less functional document than the Council of Europe specifications, also needs serious formative evaluation and review if we are really concerned with raising standards.

### The influence on media courses and textbooks

In spite of the lack of taught courses leading to the specifications, one can detect the, often unacknowledged, influence of the Council of Europe Syllabus in a number of published English language textbooks and multimedia language courses. This influence has spread beyond the original Council of Europe member states, and the specifications are reflected in course design in Africa, the Far East and Eastern Europe, particularly with respect to the teaching of English and French.

One indirect route of influence has been via the British Council/BBC multimedia course *Follow Me*. The course writers for *Follow-Me* worked in close collaboration with the Council of Europe team to help develop their highly successful course, which been used internationally, with its largest audience figures being in China. Nevertheless, the further one gets from London, the less culturally appropriate is any course designed in London for a European audience, and the further one gets from 1975, the less culturally appropriate is the course content anywhere in the world. *Follow Me* still contains some efficient language teaching and exerts a powerful fascination for beginners, but it provides a stereotypical picture of an all-white, sexist, hard-drinking culture where criminals are harmless comic figures. Presentation is, of course, tongue in check, but the wryness is often lost on the non-native speaker.

Where cultures have found the overtones of *Follow-Me* unacceptable, they have sometimes transferred the linguistic content to other courses they have devised. In Sri Lanka, for instance, the showing of *Follow-Me* on TV, was followed by the development of locally written and produced television and radio English courses (*Mayuri* and *Happy Hotel*), both with a local cultural flavour but essentially covering the same linguistic elements as *Follow Me*. That is to say they were based (fairly indirectly) on the Council of Europe specifications even though the authors may have had no direct awareness of this.

## Tests and Examinations

Another indirect route of influence has been via examination syllabuses that have themselves used it. Again, surprisingly, Examination Boards rarely mention the Council of Europe specifications overtly in their syllabuses or exam prospectuses, even when they have been influenced by them.

Notable exceptions are University of Cambridge Local examinations Syndicate's (UCLES) examinations *Key English Test* (to be introduced in 1994) and *Preliminary English Test*. These examinations test for *Waystage* and *Threshold Level* respectively. PET was taken by 37,100 students in 1992, which indicates that there exist courses working to the specifications. From 1994, both examinations will be linked to the new multimedia course *Look Ahead*, a collaborative venture of UCLES, BBC English, The British Council and Longman ELT.

The specifications, both of *Waystage* and *Threshold Level*, provide a useful basis for the design of testing systems for English. The University of Warwick, for example, worked for three years (1991-93) in collaboration with the Department of Examinations in Sri Lanka, developing tests for non-formal sector language learners (mainly adults following radio and TV English courses). The Council of Europe specifications (1975 edition) were relied on extensively for this purpose and, with some exceptions, found to be extremely 'user-friendly'.

In spite of all this activity, there has been little direct testing of learners' attainment of the specifications within Europe. One might have imagined a series of *Threshold Level Tests* in all the European languages, with course books leading to them, especially since the original specifications were for a Unit-Credit System for Languages in Europe.

To the best of my knowledge, little progress has been made towards establishing the original aim of a 'unit credit system'. What 'a system of equivalences' between different European languages would look like is still obscure. The original idea was explained by Wilkins, 1972:1:

> The language material to be learned will be organised into units and a
> learner will be awarded a specified number of credits on completion of
> each unit.... Each learner will be free to follow units which are relevant to
> the particular purposes to which he (sic) intends to put the language. The
> general aim is therefore to identify the units in behavioural terms.

This part of the project remains to be developed, and it is not hard to
envisage the problems that would arise in seeking to establish the
'units'. The unit-credit system is not mentioned in Van Ek and Trim
(1992a, 1992b) or in Trim (1992) and appears to have been dropped as a
objective, but without explanation. Is the change a result of the
problems of implementation without proper funding for research and
development? Or is it a result of unreported failures in attempts at
implementation?

To set up an actual system of testable equivalences, exam boards
from different European countries would need to co-operate in
innovative ways, and it may be that the advantages of such a project
would not warrant the time and effort required.

## School Curriculum

One major factor in the original work was that it was planned with the
adult learner exclusively in mind; the full title of the 1975 edition was
*The Threshold Level in a European Unit-Credit System for Modern
Language Learning by Adults*. Interestingly, the full title has been
dropped from the current version, and, what is more, the word 'adult' is
not mentioned at all in the new documents apart from the reference to
the original work. In fact, there is even, by implication, the suggestion
that the specifications are appropriate for secondary school students for
the authors write:

> A further criticism frequently heard was the absence of cultural content
> felt by many to be an important aspect of the contribution which the study
> of a modern language has to make to a general education in lower, and
> particularly upper, secondary education. (1992:iii)

In 1976, Van Ek had made a case for an abridged and edited
*Threshold Level* as the basis for a school syllabus, but the 1975 schools
version (which also had many limitations) is ignored in the 1990 edition,
which carries an assumption that the full version is usable for children
or adults alike. There already appears to have been a strong, if
unacknowledged, influence on secondary school language syllabuses in
this country and overseas from the *Threshold Level* specifications. There
is even some (word of mouth) indication that teachers in countries like
Spain and Italy, which are introducing English to the primary school

curriculum, are looking to the *Waystage* specifications for help in course planning.

This desire to borrow from unsuitable resources is almost certainly the result of the lack of proper funding (which translates into 'time') for developing proper school syllabuses. The impression one gets is of busy teachers and curriculum advisers cobbling together syllabuses from any available source and generally relying on whatever is to hand in their attempts to bring language teaching nearer to fulfilling communicative aims. In such circumstances, it is understandable that the Council of Europe Specifications might be seen as a useful source.

Richterich and Chancerel (1977) referred to 'the pressing demand for ready-made recipes for dealing with the practical and immediate application of the system?' and bemoaned the fact that there was no time for defining 'certain indispensable theoretical assumptions.' This seems to me to be an important issue that is still with us.

The problem is that the very strengths of the *Threshold Level* stem from the fact that the specifications were, from the very first, drawn up with the needs of specific learners in mind and these learners were not school children. The original work was identified strictly with adult language learning, sponsored by the 'Out-of School Education Committee' (see, for example, Wilkins, 1972).

The consequence was that the 'General Characterization' of the system is oriented to *adults controlling their own behaviour* with respect to the foreign context. Hence, at least two thirds of the 'General Objectives' are largely irrelevant to the interests or immediate needs of school learners. A small sample of the objectives one might consider irrelevant to children's needs (not reproduced in full) is given below (numbering as in *Threshold Level*, 1991). The brackets contain examples of what 'learners should be able to do':

1.1 *Contacts with officials* [ask for the services of an interpreter and/or legal adviser]

1.1.2 *Customs officers* [understand and complete necessary documentation; answer questions concerning whether items are for commercial use]

1.1.4 *Police* [give details of any vehicle they drive]

1.2.1 *Arrangements for accommodation* [book accommodation by letter or telephone; complain about service; query bills]

With respect to *roles*, the learners' are projected as parents, professional people, travellers in charge of organizing their own journeys, employers, purchasers, people who use banks, cash cheques and play golf. These are not roles that children perform in our society (except in play) and the language for such roles will not, on the whole, assist children in making social contacts with children from the target culture, should they be lucky enough to visit them. Moreover, the specifications are imbued with an all-pervasive commercialism and materialism that we may not feel provides the best settings for a school programme.

These specifications will not, on the whole, provide young people with linguistic access to those aspects of the target culture that might come their way. Preferable areas to aim at might be:

1    Language use in education (to consider such issues as environmental education, geographical terms, animals, aspects of history in the target culture);

2    Language use in literature and the media (including poetry, cartoons, children's film and TV, songs, comics, stories, quizzes);

3    Language use in computer games and videos (many of which are available in target languages);

4    Language needed for immediate communication on matters that interest and involve children.

Another area of concern is that children should learn the language needed for making friends with other children, both in writing and face to face.

But it is not the purpose of this paper to advocate any of the components of a European syllabus for young learners. What I am asking for is a research programme, comparable to efforts that went into the *Threshold Level*, that seriously addresses the question of what might make up appropriate specifications for language learning for children in a future Europe.

There are issues of principle that should be taken into account here. The first is how to answer the question, 'What are the factors that are central to children's use of language that should be considered in the design of language learning objectives?'

The answers to such a question would entail establishing the situation and settings in which children might wish to use the language and the type of things they might wish to say or understand.

Equally significant is the opportunity that should be provided for the creative use of the target language by the child, not only for 'self-expression', but also for the management of imaginative play and the daily routine. (See also Bloor 1991).

A further question that needs careful examination is the role of reading and writing in the communicative syllabus. The focus in *Threshold Level* is essentially utilitarian and commercial. No consideration is taken of the widely held view that reading supports all language learning. Incidentally, the successful Austrian and German primary curriculum introduces reading in the foreign language from the age of five or six.

## Conclusion

As far as the teaching of languages to adults is concerned, there is no doubt that the specifications for the *Waystage* and *Threshold Level* made an important contribution to developments in Europe. I have argued here that they have not always been used with appropriate learner groups, and that many opportunities have been missed for proper implementation and evaluation.

Nevertheless, with the revised editions now available, it may not be too late for proper courses to be designed and proper evaluations to take place. The new targeted tests referred to in this paper could be useful in this process.

Finally, it is important to remember that the Council of Europe specifications were founded on the theoretical position that claims that the form of the linguistic exponent is governed by the situation of use. This principle can usefully be remembered by course designers and examiners alike.

## References

Bloor, A.M. (1991) The role of informal interaction in teaching English to young children. In B. Brumfit, J. Moon, Ray Tongue, (eds) *Teaching English to Children*. London: Collins ELT.

Ek, J.A. van and Trim, J.L. (1992) *Waystage 1990*. Strasbourg: Council of Europe Press.

Ek, J.A. van and Trim J.L. (1992) *Threshold Level 1990*. Strasbourg: Council of Europe Press.

Richterich, R, and Chancerel J. L. (1977) *Identifying the Needs of Adults Learning a Foreign Language*. Oxford: Pergamon Press.

Trim, J.L. (1992) Language teaching in the perspective of the predictable requirements of the twenty-first century. *AILA Review*, 9, 7-20.

Wilkins, D.A. (1972) *Modern Languages: The linguistic and situational content of the common core in a unit credit system*. Strasbourg: Council of Europe (Committee for Out-of-School Education and Cultural Development).

# 3   MSc Common Room Conversations: Topics and terms

*University of Edinburgh*

## Introduction

This paper represents the first step in the direction of a larger study that aims to analyse the way that the language of students enroled on Edinburgh University's MSc in Applied Linguistics was affected by their interacting over time through the MSc course and forming a discourse community. I aim to make a generalisable statement about the pragmatic nature and function of language of any group starting as strangers and becoming a discourse community.

I have chosen to focus on certain lexical and grammatical features that depend for their meaning on knowledge of the situational context of the MSc course and interactions within its duration. I hypothesise that certain 'contextualisation cues', to use Gumperz's term referring to linguistic features that contribute to the 'signalling of contextual presuppositions' (Gumperz, 1982:71), increase over time. These can be categorised as *special terms and names, general nouns and verbs*, and *exophoric reference, substitution* and *ellipsis*. My aim is to take a developmental view of the special language that evolves in this closed network group, in order to determine if the cues emerge over time in any particular order and how they relate to each other.

I hope to explain how the in-group's language could become increasingly inaccessible to an outsider to this MSc group as the number of implicit references to assumed knowledge areas grows.

I begin by reviewing the literature on the language of social groups and the indicators of intimacy. Then I will state individual hypotheses for each of the contextualisation cues to be examined in the larger study, and I will put forward general hypotheses which suggest how these cues might interrelate.

The second half of the present paper will discuss results of analysis of a pilot study on special terms used by the MSc students throughout the course.

24

Graddol, D and Thomas, S. (1994)
*Language in a Changing Europe,*
Clevedon: BAAL and Multilingual Matters

# Review of the Literature

It appears that no study has followed through the interactions of a group of people as they become a discourse community, to discover exactly how and when grammatical and lexical reference to shared knowledge develops over time. Swales (1990) describes the academic class as forming a discourse community, defining the latter by its members' common goals, intercommunication mechanisms, particular genres and specific lexis.

> Somewhere down the line, ... understanding the rationale of and facility with appropriate genres will develop, control of technical vocabulary in both oral and written contexts will emerge (Swales 1990:32).

Our MSc students fulfil all his criteria.

Some studies have described the language of social groups but they lack a suggestion of how exactly language changes to become the language of the social group. Bernstein simply said that the features of restricted code 'interact cumulatively and developmentally reinforce each other' (Bernstein, 1971:43).

Our MSc students develop a restricted code in the sense that it is context-dependent and contains unspoken assumptions. The university students in Levy's (1979) study talked about their selected course subjects in such a way that even the staff found it difficult to understand. However, our students' language also contains elements of elaborated code: their lexis can be rational and abstract.

Kreckel (1981) describes the language of university students in terms of product rather than process, as 'a multitude of in-group codes, discipline specific and social group specific...taking discipline or group-specific knowledge for granted' (Kreckel 1981:36).

Those sociolinguists and psycholinguists who have considered how assumed knowledge areas and language change over time interdependently, refer to the change in superficial terms. Gumperz (1982) does not explore his 'contextualisation cues' (prosodic features, formulaic expressions, sequencing strategies and lexis and syntax) in depth.

Tannen (1984, 1989), describing high involvement style of those who regularly interact, mentions signals such as ellipsis and indirectness, playful routines and irony, reference to familiar jokes, yet makes no suggestion of the route from the low to the high involvement stage.

The present longitudinal study was undertaken to provide a systematic model for describing and hopefully predicting the process of language changes over time as individuals form a discourse community.

# The Study of Cues: The full study

## Hypotheses.

It is not only the background knowledge that can make a closed social network's conversations exclusive to an outsider to the group, but also the fact that the group members refer to that situational context in a particular way using contextualisation cues of reference, substitution and ellipsis, special terms and names and general words. I hypothesise that as shared knowledge grows, the intertextual frequency and textual density of contextualisation cues increases and that the language of in-group members has more contextualisation cues than that of strangers. Although the model in Figure 1 is my own, most of the classifications are taken from Halliday and Hasan (1976).

| LEXIS | GRAMMAR |
|---|---|
| Special terms | Exophoric reference |
| - technical | - existential |
| - course-related | - demonstrative |
| - specific | - comparative |
| - general | Exophoric substitn/ellipsis |
| - superordinate | - nominal |
| Course-by-context terms | - verbal |
| Proper nouns/names | - unfinished |
| General words | sentences |
| - nouns | |
| - verbs | |

*Figure 1*     *Contextualisation cues: indicators of in-group membership*

I devised four categories for the common background knowledge that would seem to be assumed by my subjects.

K1    is general knowledge of the world, including Edinburgh and the University;

K2    is general knowledge of linguistics and language teaching;

K3    is knowledge of the Department of Applied Linguistics and the Institute for Applied Language Studies in terms of the organisation typical of any MSc year;

K4    is knowledge of this particular MSc year.

*Topics* in these four areas can be grouped in two macro-categories: course-related (*c topics*) and non-course-related (*n-c topics*). K2 to K4 always contain c topics. K1 topics are generally n-c.

I hypothesise that c topics will be more impenetrable to an outsider than n-c topics. I predict that with time, c topics will be more frequent than n-c topics, and that this will cause the conversations to have larger impenetrable sections because of both the assumed knowledge area and the number of occurrences and density of contextualisation cues.

I now propose to state the individual hypotheses for each contextualisation cue. The first set of contextualisation cues is lexical: I hypothesise that there will be an increase in *special terms* (technical and course-related) and terms that are *course-related by context*, as shared knowledge grows; that the percentage of special terms out of all nouns in K2-K4 will increase over time.

The second type of lexical cue is that of *proper nouns* and *names of people*. I hypothesise that there will be an increase in the general use of names of people referring elliptically to something other than the people named, such as in the following example:

JAN 13: 'I haven't done any *Chomsky*.'

The third type of lexical cue is exophoric general words. I hypothesise that course-related words will be substituted increasingly by general words.

JAN 13: 'I've *done* all the *people*.'

Moving on to grammar, the fourth set of contextualisation cues is *exophoric reference*. I predict an increase in the percentage of exophoric third person existential pronouns and possessives out of all third person personals; an increase in demonstrative pronouns referring to course-related referents;

JAN 20: 'I mean you know what *she's* like.'

in the percentage of definite noun phrases on first mention: 'the' (non-generic) with special terms (K2-K4) and general nouns, out of all noun phrases;

NOV 7: 'So you've got *the* whole damn thing to do.'

and in the percentage of exophoric comparative reference out of all comparative reference.

JAN 13: 'I feel *more* comfortable with the data stuff.'

The fifth set of contextualisation cues to be studied is *exophoric substitution and ellipsis*. There will be an increase in the percentage of nominal exophoric substitution out of all substitution. Ellipsis can be seen in certain aspects of special terms, as I have shown. I hypothesise that there will be an increase in an extreme form of substitution: the noun phrase with vague category identifiers or sentences tailing off in vague expressions (Channell 1985) such as 'and so on' and 'and things like that'; and an increase in ellipsis in its extreme form of the unfinished sentence.

JAN 20: 'So that if you don't get it...'

As all these contextualisation cues increase, there will be a *decrease in post-head dependents* (modifiers and peripheral dependents), a reduction in restrictive modification as the bald noun-phrase becomes all that is necessary to identify the referent.

MAY 12: 'Your CV and your proposal.'

My general hypothesis about the contextualisation cues is that initially there will be a peak of special terms, proper names, demonstrative and comparative reference, combined with a drop in post-head dependents. As the course progresses, special terms and names will level off and there will be an increase in third person personals, exophoric substitution and ellipsis, and superordinates, general words and popular general expressions. This overall trend will be affected by events in the course: I predict minor increases in special terms around exam and portfolio dates and project deadlines.

I shall take into account two secondary but essential factors: *cohesion* and *function*. A consideration of cohesion should reveal that as reference becomes more exophoric, lexis more general, and post-head dependents more scarce, the risk of breakdowns and requests for clarification increase, especially in course-related topics.

The analysis of the function of utterances containing cues should show that the use of contextualisation cues is a generally expected unmarked means of claiming in-group membership (Levinson 1978). The interactional utterances may be an exchange of information to enlighten, an anxious test of normality, or a light-hearted relieving of tension using conversational implicature.

Two methodological questions need to be clarified. Although this paper suggests a model for analysing casual conversations, it should be emphasised that this is not an *a priori* model. The categories have been devised as a result of examining the dialogues with an ethnomethodological eye. It should also be made clear that although it is easier to examine only the lexis and grammar, a functional approach is necessary to give the findings a *raison d'être*.

## Method of data collection and analysis.

I openly made tape-recordings (total 264 minutes) of MSc student conversations in the common room of the Applied Linguistics department from 4 October until 12 May 1992. I recorded once a week over three periods of time: the first half of the first, second and third term. The conversations were spontaneous and unguided, and I kept at a distance at the moment of recording so as not to be included. Six native speakers of English who had options in common and tended to sit together in the common room consistently were eventually selected for analysis.

Once I had transcribed the recordings, I disregarded dialogues or long sections of dialogues which did not contain at least two of the six chosen speakers. For my pilot study, I randomly selected, from each day's recording, one three-minute segment in which the chosen speakers played centre stage and were not joined by non-native speakers of English. Subsequent analysis has revealed that all the data containing at least two of the chosen speakers is needed if enough examples of all the features are to be encountered.

## The Study of Special Terms

### Data analysis.

Before analysing special terms in all the data, I selected three of the three-minute segments (one from each recording period) for a pilot study. I first checked that the segments were a representative sample of the ratio of c topic: n-c topic of each period. Figure 2 shows the average both topic types in all dialogues for each period. There is a noticeable increase in c topic time and decrease in n-c topic time.

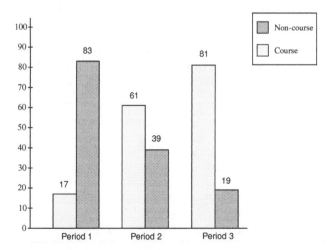

*Figure 2 Average percentage, per period, of time spent in all recorded data on course and non-course topics*

I decided to count each occurrence of a noun, even when the same noun was repeated in quick succession as a stutter. This point is especially relevant when I measure density. I calculated *lexical density* within each topic type (course-related and non-course-related).

There were three macro-categories: *special terms, course-by-context terms* and *non-course terms*. Within the macro-category special terms I made two divisions – *technical* and *course-related*. I adopted the name 'technical terms' for the category of intrinsically specialised terms independent of context, technical words of linguistics and language teaching such as 'discourse', 'creoles' and 'lesson plan'.

I used the course-related term (c term) category for terms only specialised by context, but intrinsically course-related. The category of c terms consists of *specific terms, general terms* and *superordinates*. Specific c terms were quite simply ones such as 'core project', 'portfolio' and 'topic sheet'. General c terms are count nouns usually with zero article whose precise meaning is not clear since they are the first noun of a two- or three-word phrasal expression (Huddleston 1988:103) whose second/third word(s) (often a superordinate) is omitted. Their meaning varies from context to context.

OCT 25: 'Has anybody done their *syntax*?'

Superordinate c terms substitute K2-K4 special terms, and their specific reference could be supplied by a pre-head modifier.

JAN 20: 'And *the paper'* s due in next Friday.'

The second macro-category, course-by-context term (C-cxt), was for those terms that are not intrinsically course-related but become course-related by their use in course topics, such as 'discussion' and 'this week'.

All other terms were obviously non-course-related, not even by context (n-c terms). Figure 3 shows each knowledge area with the hypothesised principal types of term that are mostly found in it. This is not to say that the other types cannot occur in each knowledge area.

|  | Special Terms | | | | C-Cxt terms | N-c terms |
|  | Technical | C Terms | | | | |
|  |  | Specific | General | Superord | | |
| K1 |  |  |  |  | X | X |
| K2 | X |  |  |  |  |  |
| K3 |  | X | X | X |  |  |
| K4 |  | X | X | X |  |  |

*Figure 3 General tendency of terms in each knowledge area.*

## Results and discussion

The number of special terms in course-related knowledge areas for each period was calculated (see Figure 4)

| Period | K2 | K3 | K4 | Total |
|---|---|---|---|---|
| Oct/Nov | 3 | 2 | 30 | 35 |
| Jan/Feb | 4 | 17 | 8 | 29 |
| Apr/May | 10 | 24 | 5 | 39 |
| Total | 17 | 43 | 43 | 103 |

*Figure 4 Total number of special terms in K2, K3, and K4.*

The number in the last period was slightly greater than that in the others, probably explained by the increase in c topics time in that period. There were twice the number of total K3 and K4 c terms than K2 technical terms.

In order to discover how each special term increases or decreases over the three periods recorded, I examined each of the two special term categories of 'technical' and 'course-related' terms individually over time. Figure 5 shows that there are more technical and specific c terms at the beginning of the course and more general and superordinate c terms at the end. This suggests that my hypothesis is confirmed.

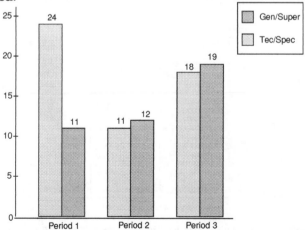

*Figure 5 Totals of special term types for each period*

Whereas all special terms in K2 are simply technical ones, special terms in K3 and K4 can be any of the c term types. In K3, they are as often specific c terms such as 'reading week', 'PhD' as superordinate c terms such as 'class', 'option', 'project'. About 20% are general c terms and in all cases they refer to courses: 'language and linguistics', 'psycho-linguistics'. K4 contains fewer superordinates (e.g. 'group', 'questions', 'books') than K3 does but the same number of general c terms, and these are in-group names and abbreviations such as 'Psycho', 'Teap', etc.

I then calculated the density of special terms and c-cxt terms in c topics and the density of n-c terms in n-c topics. By density, I mean the percentage of nouns of a particular type out of all the words in one topic type. Figure 6 shows that while special terms density remains constant, c-cxt terms increase in density. The density of n-c terms in n-c topics decreases, suggesting that while knowledge assumed in the course context is soon established, it takes longer for n-c topic knowledge to be taken-for-granted.

Finally, all these calculations must be seen against the background of the discoveries made about the increase in time spent on course topics that I explained in above. The inaccessibility of the dialogues may well be because of the greater proportion of time spent on course topics with a consistently low lexical density of special terms, which are themselves increasingly general.

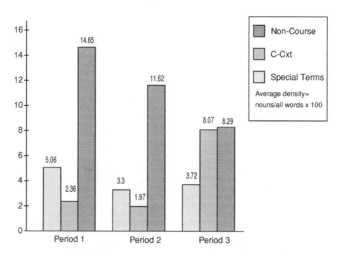

*Figure 6 Average density of various term types per period witin each topic type*

## Further research

More quantitative analyses need to be done with special terms: how they behave intertextually, and what the rest of the noun phrase contains, in each case.

In addition, special terms need to be analysed from a qualitative and functional point of view. Questions to be examined are: are special terms used as a demonstration of in-groupness or as a test of the progress of others? In the pilot study, triangulation interviews with recordees elicited global macro functional comments of an unquantifiable nature.

To facilitate such investigations, I am now analysing my dialogues on the Excel data base, tagging the text lexically and grammatically, and labelling each discourse unit for knowledge area and function.

The next stage is to calculate the percentage of each contextualisation cue per text and the density of all cues per knowledge area, in order to examine the function of discourse units with high density cues in each knowledge area.

# Conclusions

The first part of this paper offered hypotheses of a lexical and grammatical pragmatic nature about how students' language changes as a discourse community forms.

The second part of the paper consisted of a brief exploration of the first of the lexical hypotheses: that technical and specific course-related terms increase at the beginning, while general and superordinate course-related terms do not emerge and increase until half way through the course.

I hope to find pedagogical implications of the study. EAP MSc students could be helped to understand and participate in conversations between native speakers of English in their departments. They could also be trained to ascertain whether a dialogue is between strangers or between in-group members of a discourse community, by looking for the cues.

# References

Altman, I. and Taylor, D.A. (1973) *Social Penetration: the Development of interpersonal relationships.* New York: Holt Reinhart and Winston.
Argyle, M. and Trower, P. (1979) *Person to Person – Ways of communicating.* Holland: Multimedia Publications.
Berger, C. and Bradac, J. (1982) *Language and Social Knowledge.* London: Edward Arnold Ltd.
Bernstein,B.(1971) *Class, Codes and Control (Vol. I).* London:Routledge, Kegan Paul
Brown, P. and Levinson, S. (1978) *Politeness.* Cambridge: CUP.

Channell, J. (1985) *Vagueness as a Conversational Strategy*. Nottingham Linguistic Circular 14, 3-24.

Cook, G. (1989). *Discourse*. Oxford: OUP.

Coulthard, M. (1985). *An Introduction to Discourse Analysis*. London: Longman.

Giles, H. and St Clair, R. (1979) *Language and Social Psychology*. Oxford: Basil Blackwell.

Gumperz, J. (1982) *Discourse Strategies*. Cambridge: CUP.

Halliday, M. and Hasan, R. (1976) *Cohesion in English*. London: Longman.

Hinde, R. (1987) *Individuals, Relationships and Culture*. Cambridge: CUP.

Joos, M. (1967) *The Five Clocks*. New York: Harbinger Books.

Kelly, H., Bersheid E., Christensen, A. et al. (1983) *Close Relationships*. New York: W.H. Freeman and Company.

Kreckel, M. (1981) *Communicative Acts and Shared Knowledge in Natural Discourse*. London: Academic Press.

Levinson, S. (1983) *Pragmatics*. Cambridge: CUP.

Levy, D. (1979) Communicative goals and strategies: between discourse and syntax. In *Syntax and Semantics* 12, 183-210.

McCarthy, M. (1991) *Discourse Analysis for Language Teachers*. Cambridge: CUP.

Swales, J. (1990) *Genre Analysis*. Cambridge: CUP.

Tannen, D. (1984) *Conversational Style: Analyzing talk among friends*. New Jersey: Ablex Publishing Corporation.

Tannen, D. (1989) *Talking Voices*. Cambridge: CUP.

# 4 Language Preference and Structures of Code-switching

GUOWEN HUANG AND LESLEY MILROY
*University of Newcastle upon Tyne*

## Theoretical assumptions

In sociolinguistics, various approaches to code-switching (i.e., the use of two or more languages within the same conversation) are being developed. As Milroy (1987:198) observes, while some researchers are more interested in pragmatic functions and social meanings of code-switching, others are more concerned with linguistic constraints on code-switching. With respect to the latter orientation, attempts have been made to formulate linguistic constraints on switch points and different models of analysis have been proposed (see for example, Poplack, 1980; DiSciullo, Muysken and Singh, 1986; Myers-Scotton, 1992; 1993; forthcoming; Muysken, forthcoming).

Although three types of code-switching are frequently distinguished in the literature (inter-sentential, intra-sentential, and tag-switching – see Appel and Muysken, 1987:118; Romaine, 1989:112), we argue that the basic unit of analysis of spoken data should be the clause rather than the sentence (see further Huang and Milroy, 1993a; Huang, Milroy and Li, forthcoming) and therefore we shall only distinguish between two types of switching: inter-clausal switching and intra-clausal switching. We would also argue that a matrix language can be identified in every switched clause (see Huang and Milroy, 1993a; cf. Joshi 1985; Klavans, 1985; Nishimura, 1986; Appel and Muysken, 1987; Nortier, 1989; Myers-Scotton, 1992; 1993; forthcoming; Muysken, forthcoming). The matrix language, in contrast to the embedded language, provides the grammatical framework of the clauses as a whole while the embedded language typically contributes lexical materials inserted into this framework. This means that there may be two grammars interacting in the switched clause: the grammar of the matrix language and the grammar of the embedded language.

The aim of this paper is to investigate the relationships between language preference and structures of code-switching and to combine the two perspectives in a wider context of sociolinguistic studies. In the following, we shall first provide the background information of the Tyneside Chinese community. Then our analytical framework of code-

35

Graddol, D and Thomas, S. (1994)
*Language in a Changing Europe,*
Clevedon: BAAL and Multilingual Matters

switching is outlined. This will be followed by the discussion of the relationship between language preference and the structure of code-switching.

## The Tyneside Chinese community

The Chinese community in Britain is the third largest non-indigenous ethnic minority as a whole, after those of West Indian origin and from the Indian sub-continent. The Tyneside Chinese community has a population of somewhere between 5000 and 7000 (Li, 1992; Li, Milroy and Pong, 1992). The Chinese in the Tyneside community can be sub-grouped by social background or history of migration. Following Li (1992) (see also Milroy, Li and Moffatt, 1991), we would distinguish between the Chinese in the Tyneside community by looking at the history of migration and settlement:

(a)    the first generation emigrants, the grandparent generation;

(b)    the sponsored emigrants, the parent generation;

(c)    the British-born, the child generation.

Li (1992), in his study of language choice and language shift of 10 Chinese families (58 speakers) in the Tyneside Chinese community, used participant observation as the chief method of data collection with a corpus of some 23 hours of spontaneous conversation, and he analysed his linguistic data in terms of language choice at the group (community) level and code-switching at the conversational level. One of his findings suggests that the first (grandparent) generation and the second (parent) generation have a clear preference for Chinese whereas the third (child) generation has a clear preference for English in terms of language choice.

Li's finding matches the finding of a study of another 20 three generational families (which are not the same families in Li's (1992) studies) carried out by Pong (1991), who conducted a questionnaire study of language choice of the families. One of the general conclusions drawn from both Li's (1992) and Pong's (1991) studies is that the first (grandparent) and the second (parent) generations of the Tyneside Chinese community are Chinese-dominant whereas the third (child) generation is English-dominant.

## Insertional and alternational code-switching

Code-switching can be structured in two quite different ways (see Huang and Milroy, 1993b for detailed discussion; cf Joshi, 1985; Muysken, forthcoming): Alternational code-switching means that two (or more) languages are used in turn in the same clause or discourse, while insertional code-switching means that a word or a phrase from one language is put into the grammatical framework of a clause or discourse made up of another language. In conversation, both insertional and alternational code-switching can take place within a speaker's turn or between the speakers' turns. This distinction clearly relates to the matrix/embedded language distinction outlined above.

Basically, at the clausal level if the embedded element functions as a clause element, the switching is alternational. By contrast, if the embedded element plays the role of a phrase element rather than a clause element (for the distinction between a clause element and a phrase element, see Leech *et al*, 1982), the switching is insertional. Consider the following examples:

(1)    nei yeo mo dig <u>older relatives</u> a? /

(2)    nei yeo mo <u>any older relatives</u>? /

       *Do you have any older relatives?* [1, 2]

The switching in both these clauses is intra-clausal in type if examined with a view to specifying types of code-switching. However, we would argue that the switching in (1) is insertional and that in (2) is alternational because 'any older relatives' in (2) is an embedded language island (see Huang and Milroy, 1993b for detailed discussion) whereas 'older relative' in (1) is not an embedded language island (cf. Myers-Scotton, 1992;1993). The decision made here is based on the understanding that 'older relatives' in (1) alone does not function as a clause element (Leech et al, 1982) while 'any older relatives' in (2) can itself play the role of 'Object' (O) in the clause.

If we look at the well-formedness in terms of phrases functioning as clause elements, 'older relatives' in (1) is not a noun phrase (N"), but an N-prime (N') (or N-bar); only when 'older relatives' combines with its Cantonese determiner 'dig' (any) can they function as Object. By contrast, 'any older relatives' in (2) is free-standing and it is a phrase which can alone function as the Object of the verb.

The discussion so far has suggested that at the clausal level if the embedded element, which stands as an embedded language island, functions as a clause element, the structure of switching is alternational. However, if the embedded element does not function as a clause element by itself, which is not regarded as an embedded language island, the structure of switching is insertional.

At the discoursal level, the conditions for identifying the structure of code-switching are as follows:

(a)      If the matrix language of one or more of the clauses is in one code and the matrix language of one or more of the clauses is in the other code, the structure of code-switching is alternational.

(b)      If the matrix language of all the clauses in the discourse in only in one code, the structure of code-switching is insertional even if there are embedded language islands.

Conditions (a) and (b) are mutually exclusive. According to Condition (a), the structure of code-switching of Example (3) below is alternational at the discoursal level.

(3)    (A is a woman of about 35 and B is a boy of 17)

    1   A: neidei Zungguog pengyeo (.) keudei tung nei gong medye?/

    2   B: depends on / where you are / because hei Yingguog dig deifong (.) dosou gong Yingmen /

    3   A: o (.) gem dosou gong Yingmen / dimgai ne? /

    4   B: I don't know / 'cause the people in Scotland or in London (.) keudei gong dodig Yingmen / so if I talk to them / English is more convenient /

        A: What language do your Chinese friends use when they talk to you?

        B: Depends on where you [we] are, because in Britain most of us speak English.

        A:  So most of you speak English, but why?

        B: I don't know, because the people in Scotland or in London, they speak more English (than others in other places). So if I talk to them, English is more convenient

This question-answer stretch of discourse is taken from an interview. The stretch is made up of four conversational turns, two (Turn 1 and Turn 3) by the interviewer and the other two (Turn 2 and Turn 4) by the interviewee. These four turns are composed of ten clauses:

    {1}    neidei Zungguog pengyeo (.) keudei tung nei gong medye

    {2}    depends on

    {3}    where you are

    {4}    because hei Yingguog dig deifong dosou gong Yingmen

    {5}    o (.) gem dosou gong Yingmen

    {6}    dimgai ne

{7}   I don't know

{8}   because the people in Scotland or in London (.) keudei gong dodig Yingmen

{9}   so if I talk to them

{10}  English is more convenient

Of the ten clauses, five (i.e. {2}, {3}, {7}, {9}, {10}) are made up only of English words in Turns 2 and 4 and three (i.e. {1}, {5}, {6}) are composed only of Cantonese words in Turns 1 and 2. There are only two clauses (i.e. {4} and {8}) which contain intra-clausal switching. If we look at the choice of code from the point of view of inter-speaker interaction, we can see that the interviewer (Speaker A) only uses Cantonese whereas the interviewee (Speaker B) uses both English and Cantonese. Alternative use of code takes place between the speakers' turns. Therefore, the structure of code-switching in this discourse is alternational. If we look at the choice of code from the point of view of intra-speaker production, we can see that the interviewee uses both codes alternatively. He switches to Cantonese in the middle of his speech: In his first response (Turn 2), he begins with English ('depends on where you are because...') and then switches to Cantonese in the middle of the utterance ('hei Yingguog dig deifong dosou gong Yingmen') (Clauses {2}, {3} and {4}); the same is true of his second response (Turn 4) ('I don't know / because the people in Scotland or in London (.) keudei gong dodig Yingmen') (Clauses {7} and {8}). Therefore, we may say that alternation takes place between speakers' interaction and within the same speaker's speech.

However, in the first response (Clauses {2}, {3} and {4}), the interviewee begins in English and finishes in Cantonese. The direction of switching between Turn 1 and Turn 2 (and within Turn 2) is first from Cantonese to English and then from English to Cantonese, as is represented below:

TURN 1 **Cantonese** ('neidei Zungguog pengyeo (.) keudei tung nei gong medye' /) =>TURN 2 **English** ('depends on / where you are / because') => **Cantonese** ('hei Yingguog dig deifong dosou gong Yingmen'/).

In the second question-answer turns, the direction of code-switching is first from Cantonese to English and then from English to Cantonese and finally from Cantonese to English, as is shown below:

TURN 3 **Cantonese** ('o (.) gem dosou gong Yingmen / dimgai ne' /) => TURN 4: **English** (' I don't know / because the people in Scotland or in London ' (.)) => **Cantonese** ('keudei gong dodig Yingmen') => **English** ('so if I talk to them / English is more convenient').

By contrast, in the following example, the matrix language of all the clauses is Cantonese. Therefore, according to Condition (b) above, the structure of code-switching in Example 4 below is insertional.

(4)   (The speaker is a woman of 39, who came to live in Britain when she was 20. Here she is talking (to another bilingual woman) about her way of bringing up her children)

hoyi gong deg wa / jing dou keu houqi wa disabled / soyi wa gogdeg / jing dou keu disabled / m hei jing dou keu independent / nei ji m ji a? / keu wa/ nei make keudei disabled / nei m hei love keudei / nei hei jing dou keudei handicap / which ngo gogdeg keudei gong deg ngam / keudei yeo keudeige point / keudei brought up ge / seimenzei hou independent / m tung ngodei brought up ge seimenzei / ngodei brought up ge seimenzei / ngo gogdeg / ngodei bring up ge seimenzei / yiu bei keu dodig love a /

*I can say that I have made him disabled. So I feel I have made him disabled, not made him independent, do you understand (me)? He says you make them disabled, you don't love them, and you have made them handicapped, which, I feel what they say is right; they have their point. The children they brought up [bring up] are very independent, (they are) not like the children we brought up [bring up]. The children we brought up [bring up], I think we should give more love to the children we bring up.'*

As we can see from the example, the embedded items are either single words or phrasal verbs. Clearly, all the clauses in this piece of discourse follow the Cantonese grammatical framework and the matrix language of all the clauses is Cantonese. All the switchings are intra-clausal in type. The structure of switching in Example 4 is clearly insertional.

If we take the clause as a basic unit of analysis, we can identify the structure of switching within a clause as either insertional or alternational, schematised as follows:

*Insertional*:    A[B]A or B[A]B

*Alternational*:  AB or BA

In the 'A[B]A' structure, the matrix language of the code-switched clause is Code A whereas in 'B[A]B' the matrix language of the clause is Code B. In the 'AB' structure, the direction of code-switching is from Code A to Code B while in the 'BA' structure, the direction of code-switching is from Code B to Code A. The code-switching structure of Example 1 above (repeated below) is 'A[B]A' in which Cantonese is the matrix language and that of 2 above (repeated below) is 'AB' in which the direction of code-switching is from Cantonese to English.

(1)    nei yeo mo dig <u>older relatives</u> a? /

(2 )   nei yeo mo <u>any older relatives</u>? /

*Do you have any older relatives?*

Given that a matrix language can be identified for any code-switched clause, the structure of switching in a code-switched clause can be alternational even if the matrix language is identified (see Example 2 above).

If a turn in a conversation consists of only one word or one phrase, the switching may be either 'A[B]A' or 'B[A]B' depending on which is the matrix language. If a turn consists of a clause or more than one clause, the switching at the clausal level may be insertional (i.e., 'A[B]A') or alternational (i.e., 'AB'). However, the switching at the turn-level may be very simple or complex. For example, the switching structure within the turn in Example 4 is very simple. Of the 19 clauses in this turn, five of them are monolingual (i.e., no switching takes place in them) and the other 14 code-switched clauses share the same code-switching structure 'A[B]A' in which Cantonese is the matrix language.

Examples 3 and 4 above present two different structures of code-switching. That is to say, the structure of switching in Example 3 is basically alternational whereas that of Example 4 is insertional. The difference between these two examples arises from the speaker's bilingual ability rather than from variation in the interlocutor since both Speaker B in Example 3 and the speaker in Example 4 were talking to the same person. Speaker B in Example 3 was born and brought up in Britain and his language preference is English (see Pong, 1991; Li, 1992). In other words, he is English-dominant in terms of his language preference and language behaviour.

By contrast, the speaker in Example 4 is a woman of 39, who came to live in Britain when she was 20. Her language preference is Cantonese and she is a Chinese-dominant and non-fluent bilingual (see further Huang and Milroy, forthcoming). As was pointed out earlier, the switching in her utterances in Example 4 is consistently insertional. That is to say, English items are inserted into the Cantonese grammatical framework. The switching is intra-clausal in type. The embedded items are single words or phrasal verbs. There is no inter-clausal switching in her utterances (either in Example 4 or in the rest of her utterances in our corpus, see Huang and Milroy (forthcoming) for further discussion). The degree of complexity of switching in her utterances is totally different from that of Speaker B in Example 3. To put it simply, the switching in 4 is insertional whereas the switching in Example 3 is alternational. Therefore, the language choice pattern within the turn of Example 4 can be described as 'C[E]C', whereas that in the long turns in Example 3 as 'CE' or 'EC'.

The general conclusion to be drawn from the discussion in this section is that the type of structural patterns evident in the switching is closely related to the speaker's general language preference as well as his or her bilingual competence.

The length of a turn also has an important role to play in the structure of code-switching. Although it is unlikely for the Chinese-dominant bilinguals (i.e. members of the first/grandparent and second/parent generations) to employ alternational switching even when the turn consists of more than one clause (e.g. Example 4 above), English-dominant bilinguals commonly employ the insertional structure (i.e. A[B]A) when the turn is short. Now let us look at another example:

(5)　　　(A is a woman of about 35 and B is a boy of 17, the same two participants as those in Example 3 above)

1　A. neidei <u>daytime school</u> yeo mo Zungguog tunghog a? /

2　B. yeo /

3　A. gem keu tung nei gong medye a? /

4　B. yunqun Yingmen /

5　A. yunqun Yingmen /

6　B. a (.) yeo yedgo hei (.) yeo lenggo hei / keita godig zeo <u>fifty-fifty</u> lo /

7　A. dimgai gem degyi ne? /

8　B. '<u>cause</u> yeo yedgo le / keu (/) <u>I don't know</u> (/) keu giu / keu men ngo / '<u>can you speak English</u> (.) m hei (.) <u>Chinese fluently?</u>' / <u>I said yes</u> / ngo men fan keu / keu <u>just said</u> / '<u>not really</u>' a / <u>so it means</u> / <u>it was best to speak in English with him</u> / <u>but the majority of Chinese people within that (.) college</u> le (.) zeo <u>fifty-fifty</u> gem /

1　A. Do you have any Chinese school-mates at your daytime school?

2　B. Yes.

3　A. What language does he speak to you?

4　B. Completely English.

5　A. Completely English.

6　B. Oh, there is one, there are two [who always speak English to me]; others use <u>fifty</u> [English and] <u>fifty</u> [Chinese].

7　A. Why so strange?

8　B. <u>Because</u> there was one, he, I don't know, he called, he asked me, 'Can *you speak English, no, Chinese fluently?' I said 'yes'; then I asked him and he just said 'not really'; so it means it was best to speak in English with him; but [as to] the majority of Chinese people within that college, / [we speak] fifty [English and] fifty [Chinese].*

The participants of this interaction are the same as those in Example (3). In this interaction, Speaker B has four conversational turns. When the turns are short (i.e. Turn 2 and 4), he uses only Cantonese to accommodate to the other participant's language preference. However, when the turn becomes a bit longer (i.e., Turn 6), he makes one insertion (i.e. 'fifty-fifty'). And when the turn consists of more than two clauses, he switches from English to Cantonese and then the other way round. Structurally speaking, the switching in Turn 8 is both insertional and alternational.

# Discussion

Following our examination of code-switched utterances by Chinese/English bilinguals in the Tyneside Chinese community, we would propose to make a distinction between the Chinese-dominant bilinguals (i.e., mainly members of the parent/second generation, since almost all the members of the grandparent/first generation are monolingual) and the English-dominant bilinguals in the Tyneside Chinese community. The distinction can be made with respect to (a) the general structure of code-switching, (b) the issue of identifying the matrix language, (c) the size of the embedded language item and (d) the question of whether these speakers use two languages or three languages. We shall look at each of these issues in turn.

(a)    As was already pointed out earlier, the Chinese-dominant bilinguals usually make use of only insertional code-switching, both at the clausal level and discoursal level. By contrast, the English-dominant bilinguals usually use alternational switching, especially when they are interacting with members of the parent generation and members of their own generation. Therefore, for members of the parent generation, the direction of switching is usually from Chinese to English. On the other hand, for members of the child generation, the direction of switching can be either way, depending on who they are talking to and how long and complex the turn is.

(b)    Mixed utterances by members of the parent generation usually follow the Chinese grammatical framework. That is to say, a matrix language can be identified in code-switched utterances at both the clausal level and the discoursal level (Huang, Milroy and Li forthcoming). By contrast, it is often very difficult to convincingly identify the matrix language of the mixed utterances by members of the British-born generation (cf. Huang and Milroy 1993a). This is the case particularly when the conversation is spontaneous and when the turn of the conversation consists of more than two clauses.

(c)     As is clear in our corpus, in the mixed utterances by the Chinese-dominant bilinguals, the embedded language (i.e., English) items are usually single words or short phrases (Huang and Milroy forthcoming). The switching is intra-clausal in type. On the other hand, the embedded language (both Chinese and English) items by the British-born Chinese can be words, phrases and clauses, depending on the nature and interlocutor of the conversation. The switching can be both intra-clausal or inter-clausal in type.

(d)     With respect to members of the Chinese-dominant generation, we can reasonably say that these bilinguals use two grammars in their production (cf. Myers-Scotton, 1992; 1993). That is, the Chinese grammar provides the general syntactic framework and the English grammar governs the syntax of the embedded items. However, with respect to members of the English-dominant generation, the situation is more complex in that there may be said to be three different grammars in operation at different times. These three grammars are: the Chinese grammar, the English grammar and the code-switching grammar (cf Sankoff and Poplack, 1981). However, it may be argued that there is only one grammar (i.e. the code-switching grammar) for some members of the British-born Chinese because they are unable to keep the two languages separate, especially in spontaneous conversation and when the turn of the conversation is made up of more than two clauses.

We may note in conclusion that although these two perspectives are usually kept separate in the research literature, structural constraints on code-switching are closely related to patterns of language shift and language maintenance in the bilingual community. Furthermore, bilinguals with different degrees of language preference and language proficiency employ different structures and skills of code-switching. Our structural analysis of code-switching provides further support for the hypothesis that the Tyneside Chinese community is undergoing a process of language shift from Chinese to English with different structural manifestations of bilingual behaviour constituting tansitional stages (Milroy and Li, 1990; Li, 1992; Li, Milroy and Pong, 1992).

## Acknowledgements

This is a revised version of the paper presented at the Annual Meeting of BAAL held in Salford in September 1993. We would like to thank participants of our presentation who not only expressed their interest in our work but also made useful comments. The mixed language data presented in this paper are taken from a 30-hour corpus of Cantonese/English conversation. The data were collected by Li Wei and Pong Sin Ching and the examples used in this paper were transcribed by

Huang Guowen. The work reported here is part of a larger investigation of the bilingual language behaviour of the Chinese community in the North East of England which has received support from the Economic and Social Research Council (Grants R000221074 and R000232956), the Nuffield Foundation (Small Grants Scheme) and the Research Committee, University of Newcastle upon Tyne. This assistance is gratefully acknowledged.

## Notes

1    The notation of the romanised system for transcribing spoken Cantonese is according to Yiu et al (1983), with tones suppressed. Within the example, '(.)' indicates a pause and '/' indicates a clause boundary.

2    In this paper, the English part in the code-switched example is underlined. This does not in any sense suggest that English is the embedded or matrix language in the example. Translations into English are italicised.

# References

Appel, R. and Muysken, P. (1987) *Language Contact and Bilingualism*. London: Edward Arnold.

DiSciullo, A.M., Muysken, P. and Singh, R. (1986) Government and code-mixing. *Journal of Linguistics* 22, 1-24.

Huang, G.W. and Milroy, L. (1993a) *Evaluating Ways of Identifying the Matrix Language in Code-switching with Cantonese/English Examples*. Department of Speech, University of Newcastle upon Tyne. (Unpublished manuscript)

Huang, G.W. and Milroy, L. (1993b) *The Structure of Code-switching: An analytical framework for the study of alternational and insertional code-switching with Cantonese/English examples*. Department of Speech, University of Newcastle upon Tyne. (Unpublished manuscript)

Huang, G.W. and Milroy, L. (forthcoming) Language choice and code-switching behaviour: A case study in the Tyneside Chinese community. *Newcastle University Studies in Language and Speech*. Series A.

Huang, G.W., Milroy, L. and Li, W. (forthcoming). A two-level analysis of identifying the matrix language in Cantonese/English code-switching. *Newcastle University Studies in Language and Speech*. Series A.

Joshi, A. (1985) Processing of sentence with intra-sentential code-switching. In D. Dowty, L. Kartunen, and A. Zwicky (eds) *Natural Language Processing: Psychological, computational and theoretical perspectives*. Cambridge: Cambridge University Press.

Klavans, J.L. (1985) The syntax of code-switching: Spanish and English. In L.D. King, and C.A. Maley, (eds) *Selected Papers from the XIIIth Linguistic Symposium on Romance Languages*. Amsterdam: Benjamins, pp.213-231.

Leech, G., Deuchar, M. and Hoogenraad, R. (1982) *English Grammar for Today*. London: Macmillan.

Li, W. (1992) *Language Choice and Language Shift in a Chinese Community in Britain*. Unpublished PhD thesis, University of Newcastle upon Tyne.

Li, W., Milroy, L. and Pong, S.C. (1992) A two-step sociolinguistic analysis of code-switching and language choice: The example of a bilingual Chinese community in Britain. *International Journal of Applied Linguistics* 2/1, 63-87.

Luedi, G., Milroy, L., and Muysken, P. (eds) (forthcoming). *One Speaker, Two Languages: Cross-disciplinary perspectives on code-switching.* Strasbourg: European Science Foundation.

Milroy, L. (1987) *Observing and Analysing Natural Language.* Oxford: Blackwell.

Milroy, L. and Li, W. (1990) *A Sociolinguistic Investigation of Language Shift in Chinese communities in the North East of England.* End of Award Report to ESRC (R000221074).

Milroy, L., Li, W. and Moffatt, S. (1991) Discourse patterns and fieldwork strategies in urban settings. *Journal of Multilingual and Multicultural Development* 12/4, 287-300.

Muysken, P. (forthcoming) Code-switching and grammatical theory. In Luedi, Milroy and Muysken (eds.).

Myers-Scotton, C. (1992). Comparing codeswitching and borrowing. *Journal of Multilingual and Multicultural Development* 13/1&2, 19-39.

Myers-Scotton, C. (1993) *Duelling Languages: Grammatical structure in codeswitching.* Oxford: Clarendon Press.

Myers-Scotton, C. (forthcoming) A lexically-based production model of codeswitching. In Luedi, Milroy and Muysken (eds.).

Nishimura, M. (1986) Intrasentential code-switching: The case of language assignment. In J. Vaid (ed.) *Language Processing in Bilinguals: Psycholinguistic and neuropsychological perspectives.* Hillsdale, NJ: Lawrence Erlbaum Associates.

Nortier, J. (1990) *Dutch-Moroccan Arabic Code Switching Among Moroccans in the Netherlands.* Dordrecht: Foris.

Pong, SC. (1991) *Intergenerational Variation in Language Choice Patterns in a Chinese Community in Britain.* Unpublished M.Phil thesis, University of Newcastle upon Tyne.

Poplack, S. (1980) Sometimes I'll start a sentence in Spanish Y TERMINO EN ESPANOL: Toward a typology of code-switching. *Linguistics* 18, 581-616.

Romaine, S. (1989). *Bilingualism.* Oxford: Basil Blackwell.

Sankoff, D. and Poplack, S. (1981). A formal grammar for code-switching. *Papers in Linguistics* 14/1, 3-45.

Yiu, B.C. (1983). *Guongzeoyem Jidin (A Dictionary of Cantonese).* Guongzeo: Guongdung Yenmen Cedbanse (Guangzhou: Guangdong People's Press).

# 5   Discourse Context as a Predictor of Grammatical Choice

REBECCA HUGHES, RONALD CARTER and MICHAEL MCCARTHY
*University of Nottingham*

## Introduction

Our aim in this work could be seen as part of the move to rehabilitate the teaching of grammar in the EFL classroom – a process which has never ceased, but which has been somewhat marginalised by the more politically correct emphasis on communicative competence. In particular, we are concerned with providing materials which take into account the practical realities of teaching situations: classrooms where the numbers may be greater than would be ideal, self-study where no native speaker may be available as a resource and so on. We shall be discussing the theoretical framework later in this paper. Suffice it to say at this stage that our theory is largely driven by a concern to produce materials of the type just described, to base our linguistic description (where possible) on language of the type actually used rather than idealisations, and to consider the pedagogic benefits of looking at grammar from the point of view of contexts beyond the sentence.

Despite the title of this paper, our aims are rather modest and pragmatic. We not attempting to describe the workings of whole of the English language. We are not attempting to cover all areas of grammar for the learner of English. In general, we hope to point to useful correlations between appropriate structures and particular contexts, and provide examples of ways of applying some of the findings of discourse analysis to classroom materials.

The main assumptions behind the approach are:

1   Grammar can be seen as a set of skills, rather than a body of knowledge. As such, the teaching of grammar need not be at odds with the communicative approach, but rather should complement it.

2   There are distinct areas of grammatical choice available to a native speaker which are strongly affected by the nature of the surrounding discourse.

47

Graddol, D and Thomas, S. (1994)
*Language in a Changing Europe,*
Clevedon: BAAL and Multilingual Matters

3    In terms of practical pedagogy, not all grammatical features lend
     themselves to being understood by learners in the same way. In
     particular, some features can only be internalised and produced
     appropriately when seen from within the discourse context.

We shall deal with each of these areas in a little more detail, below.

## Grammar as a set of skills

Rather than approaching the teaching of grammar as the conveying of
information about a set of rules governing language, we take as our
premise the idea that grammar can be seen as a set of inter-related and
interdependent skills. An initial tripartite categorisation of these could
be the following:

1    Conscious and analytic aspects that can usefully be taught at sentence or
     clausal level, and about which the standard grammar of English offers
     no choice, for example, subject verb agreement.

2    Discourse related areas of grammatical choice, where understanding the
     issues involved in appropriate use of structures may depend on the
     larger linguistic context in which the choice is made, for example,
     understanding the formulaic nature of closings.

3    Pragmatic skills which enable the learner to reach full grammatical
     competence in terms of applying accurate and appropriate structures in
     a way that is acceptable in a given socio-cultural and discourse setting.

The distinction between discoursal choice and pragmatic skills is not
clear cut. An eventual definition of the relationship may show the
former as being one, key, area of pragmatic competence. And, we hope,
an area that is more readily taught than the latter. Discourse analysis
suggests a degree of predictability in language, at a level higher than
the sentence.

Whilst these areas of grammar have been separated out for
descriptive purposes, this should in no way be seen as suggesting a
division in terms of progress through an ideal syllabus. At present, the
first and third areas appear to be given greater prominence. That is to
say, materials are available which encourage the accurate practice of
particular structures, say passive constructions. Similarly, in the
functional or communicative syllabus pragmatic issues such as formal
versus informal address are presented. However, without a bridging
skill which enables them to manipulate structures within a discourse
context, too large a cognitive leap is perhaps demanded of learners.

# Defining the discourse context

Defining linguistically significant context is not easy. However, the main thrust of the theoretical framework underpinning our approach is that insufficient context for meaningful grammar choice is provided by a sentence/clause-complex level analysis. That is to say, a particular grammatical structure, in many cases, becomes inappropriate only in the context of the preceding and subsequent discourse, for example, see McCarthy (1994) on the choice between *it*, *this* and *that* for referring to segments of discourse.

It is in this somewhat negative and loose sense (i.e. not sentence level) that we are taking the term discourse context at present. The significant context may range from macro level, such as spoken versus written channel, to relatively micro level contexts, such as communicative function or textual organisation.

# Discourse versus sentence approaches

As will be seen from the foregoing discussion, we are attempting to combine theoretical and practical elements, which we see as inextricably linked to one another. In terms of theory, we are discussing the correlation between discourse context and particular grammatical features, for example, contrasts in the level and nature of subordination in spoken and written material; patterns of ellipsis in casual conversation; the functions of conditional clauses in differing conditions. Such features, we suggest, are a resource available to native speakers in both comprehension and production. The most clear cut example is newspaper headlines, where the distinctive grammatical constructions make them instantly recognisable, both in and out of their graphical context. Such language, with its frequent deletion of articles, auxiliaries, and verb *to be* and its distinctive signalling of tense, is usually held up as an idiosyncratic and isolated area of language. However, other discourse may similarly restrict grammatical choice, if to a lesser extent, if the language used is to fit with the expected norms. A case in point would be the low frequency of personal pronouns and the relatively high frequency of passive constructions in formal academic writing.

However, at a more practical level, we are most interested in those areas where structural/sentence based grammars appear insufficient for learners and teachers, rather than in describing the grammatico-stylistic features of the whole of The Language (whatever that may be). This practical limitation on our field of study in turn raises theoretical questions: which features are appropriate for sentence based approaches, and why? Two initial answers suggest themselves. Firstly, those aspects of language, particularly found in the spoken mode, which have not been fully described. Secondly, those aspects of traditional grammars which reflect essential features of the language (for example, word order in noun groups, the use of articles and so on) but which teachers feel are difficult to get across to learners.

To summarize, we would like to isolate distinct aspects of grammar which are influenced by their discourse context, and we are particularly interested in the subset of those aspects which may be the *bêtes noires* of EFL teachers. This subset, we suggest, may lend itself to being taught through a more discourse based approach.

We shall return to this below, but would now like to contextualize our work a little more.

## Previous discourse and text-based approaches to grammar.

The idea of approaching grammar teaching from the angle of something other than a sentence based model of language use is hardly new, or, by now particularly contentious. However, we are suggesting that previous approaches have, in fact, been deeply influenced by two factors which to some extent limit their usefulness in the classroom. In the final analysis, any judgment as to 'correctness' tends to resort to the grammar of standard, written English. This is unsurprising given the difficulties of describing the less fixed and capturable regularities of non-standard and/or spoken English, together with the monumental presence of grammars such as the Quirk 'Comprehensive'. Furthermore, as mentioned above, some forms which are produced by native speakers of standard English on a daily basis, have not been fully described in more discourse-oriented grammars. For example subject deletion in interactive conversation (a: *has the post been?* b: *haven't looked yet*), or complement fronting (*helpful would be if you gave me an answer today*), extended disjuncts (*brilliant action tonight eight gold medals will be won*), or progressive forms on apparently 'forbidden' verbs: *The office are going to be wanting marks by December*) and so on. All these examples were attested recently, and are not unusual types of construction, since similar ones can be heard daily, used by speakers of standard English. Nevertheless, little help with the teaching of them can be found in present grammars and classroom materials.

### Functional/notional approaches

The conception of grammar as the correct encoding of a series of separate functions removes the problem of the sentence to the realm of psychology. Even allowing that the set of functions to be encoded by a language could be isolated, the potential for realisation is a non-finite set, and the function to utterance relation ceases to be a helpful one. In pedagogic terms, the approach can present a complex new level of comprehension for the learner, that is to say, understanding the functional concept being presented and 'translating' this with reference to a student's own cultural belief and behaviour system.

## Text-based approaches, including corpus linguistics

The 'clue/signal' approach perpetuates the concept of discrete grammatical elements which can be abstracted from their context, and learned in isolation. In the classroom, the tendency is for texts to be 'mined' for the particular feature required by the syllabus or unit.

A classic example of this can be found in materials produced by one of the present authors in McCarthy et al's *Proficiency Plus – grammar, lexis, discourse* published in the mid-eighties, and more recently Alexander's 1993 *Longman's Advanced Grammar*, reference and practice shows the same approach. In both real and/or realistic texts are presented as the basis of a set of grammatical points to note and related practice exercises. However, once extracted from the text, little comment is made of the significance of the structures in relation to surrounding discourse, for example, the position in the organisation of the text or the importance of topic foregrounding. Without the realisation of the importance of such matters, learners are handicapped from the moment they are introduced to a structure, in terms of appropriate usage.

The difference in our work is mainly that of focus. Texts, both spoken and written, are seen as a complex system of interdependent lexical and grammatical features. The choice of these is, we suggest, motivated by both function and local context.

## Communicative approaches

In recent years the fashion for communicative approaches has waxed and waned as research has suggested that accuracy is not an inevitable by- product of attempts at communication in the target language. As suggested above, the skill versus knowledge dichotomy is not one which we wish to perpetuate. The aim is to integrate tasks which foster accuracy into the framework of a communicative syllabus, rather than falling back on the atomization of grammatical structures learned in isolation at sentence level.

# Structural versus discourse approaches

**Features which lend themselves to a sentence/structure based approach.**

Earlier, when describing grammar teaching in the light of a set of interrelated skills, we touched on the notion of areas of the language which may lend themselves/be most appropriately taught by means of a sentence level approach, and contrasted them against other areas which did not. We suggested that it may be fruitful to look at areas of grammar in which teachers feel that there is a need for more materials and/or are dissatisfied with the grammatical descriptions available to them at present, and to analyze them from a contextualised discourse level, rather than at sentence level. We shall now briefly consider some of the areas which may fall into these different categories.

For ease of reference we shall give the two types of feature the loose titles of 'structural' and 'discoursal' (though these terms are perhaps misleading given their history in academic circles). In the former category come such features as subject verb agreement, the formation of the tenses, number, in effect the relatively fixed and restricted set of choices that constitute closed systems. The patterns of correct combinations represented lend themselves to a somewhat mundane, learning- (as opposed to acquisition) based approach at the sentence level. Furthermore, in our experience, (and see Hammerley, 1991; Celce-Muria, 1991) there does not appear to be enough semantic loading of these features in a communicative setting for learners to feel the need to produce accurate constructions. That is to say, a learner will probably be understood if he/she produces *he go to London many time* despite losing the nuance of the difference between *he goes/he has been/he has gone*.

## Discourse oriented features

The most obvious starting point for a discourse grammar is features which are by nature connected to preceding or ensuing items in the discourse. Among these are the realisations of endophoric and exophoric reference; elliptical constructions; conjuncts and disjuncts. Secondly, there are the related areas where grammatical choice is influenced by the state of focus of a particular topic. For example, the use of articles; defining and non- defining relative clauses; adverbial fronting; ordering of main and subordinate clauses, and so on. In addition, the appropriate use of particular aspects of the language may relate to discourse context. For example, tense, aspect and voice choices. A brief example follows in the area of the use of articles in order to support the notion that grammar in discourse context involves an element of choice between structures, and that these choices do not always map on to the traditional grammatical divisions we have been used to dealing with in language pedagogy.

We might teach possessive pronouns at one stage in a syllabus, contrasting *my dog, our dog, their dog* and articles at a different point, contrasting *a dog, the dog, dogs*. If, on the basis of this, we then ask students the following:

> Which person would you ask these questions to? (a neighbour/ a stranger/ a member of the family)
>
> a) Have you seen the dog?
>
> b) Have you seen our dog?
>
> c) Have you seen a dog?

The second (*our dog*) would seem to be the obvious candidate for being asked to 'a member of the family', rather than, as is more likely to be the case to 'a stranger'. Such interconnections and contrasts only become accessible to be learned as potential choices when structures are placed in a context.

Since this is a work in progress report, we now turn to some sample materials in order to flesh out the approach, rather than dwell on defining the set of features we may eventually be dealing with, this set being somewhat fluid at present.

# Some products of this approach

The method adopted in the materials is strongly inductive, an approach which we feel can go some way towards bridging the gap between the communicative – structural dichotomy outlined above. That is to say, the task based, and interactive nature of the materials places the onus on the student to reason, infer, and/or test their own intuitions before generalisations and explanations are given. This in turn makes possible the generation of individual learning patterns, and active acquisition, within the context of what would normally be a teacher centred environment (i.e. the large class).

### Ellipsis

1)   Look at this extract from a tape-recording of people speaking. Sometimes you may feel there are words 'missing', things you would normally expect to find if people followed the 'rules' of written English grammar. Underline places where you feel the speakers have reduced what they are saying. What would they have said in full if they had put in all the necessary

written grammar? How formal do you think these situations are?

[A is telling B what route he took in his car to get to where they are speaking]

A: And I came over Mistham by the reservoirs, nice it was. B: Oh, by Mistham, over the top, nice run. A: Colours are pleasant, aren't they? B: Yeah. A: Nice run, that.

*The future*

2)    Here is a bit of a real conversation recorded in a shoe-shop. The customer is worried about the shoes being too tight. He hopes they will 'ease up' (become looser). Why do you think he and the assistant use a different form for the future?

Assistant: You always get that with high, er, first time, you know.

Customer: Is that going to ease...?

Assistant: It will definitely ease up.

3)    This is a short extract from a real conversation between a group of friends who are just about to leave the house to go for a drink. Do you think Faye has:

(a) already decided to 'break' (ie start spending) her twenty pound note?

(b) has not decided, and will only break it if someone wants a drink?

Faye: I'm going to break a twenty pound note, if anyone wants a drink.

What would it have meant if she had used will break?

# References

Celce-Murcia, M. (1991) Language and communication: a time for equilibrium and integration. In: *Georgetown University Round Table on Languages and Linguistics*, 1991. Washington University Press.

Hammerley, H. (1991) *Fluency and Accuracy*. Clevedon: Multilingual Matters.

McCarthy, M. (1994) *It, this* and *that*. In R.M. Coulthard (ed.) *Advances in Written Text Analysis*. London: Routledge.

# 6 West German Banks and East German Consumers: A study in inter-cultural advertising communication

HELEN KELLY
*Aston University*

## Introduction

This paper concerns research of which the objective is to design a model of inter-cultural advertising communication based on the situation in the new federal states in Germany, or what is perhaps more commonly known as the former German Democratic Republic (GDR). Even before formal unification, an article entitled 'Einfach lächerlich' in the magazine 'Der Spiegel' had drawn attention to the frustrations and numerous pitfalls confronting West German advertisers in their endeavours to win over customers in the former GDR. To their astonishment, they discovered that not only did East German consumers not understand many of the terms used in the advertisements, but they did not like the approach, finding it loud and obtrusive, seductive and decadent, often sexist and above all comical – even coining the term *Schickimicki Werbung* to describe it.

West German researchers were baffled by the fact that an adjective like *aprilfrisch* which has a very positive association with the West German consumer was neutral to the East German. They were forced to acknowledge that the *Ostmensch* or East German is different – ideologically, socially, culturally, economically and linguistically – and that a separate *Kommunikationsgemeinschaft* had indeed existed in the former GDR.

This unique situation provides an excellent case study for investigating the subtleties of inter-cultural advertising communication. I chose the banking industry, because banks, being the very backbone of western-style capitalism would have to overcome certain image problems in the former GDR; also, the understanding of what a bank is and does is very much influenced by the political ideology and economic orientation of the particular country in which it operates; and, furthermore, from a linguistic point of view, the language of

55

Graddol, D and Thomas, S. (1994)
*Language in a Changing Europe,*
Clevedon: BAAL and Multilingual Matters

banking and bank advertising in West Germany has, in recent years, been expanded by neologisms, internationalisms and Fremdwörter (e.g. das Leasing, das Electronic Banking etc).

Initially, I shall discuss the model which I have derived based on Sperber and Wilson's relevance theory and then go on to apply the two main criteria of the model – needs and cultural knowledge – to a sample advertisement in order to highlight the possible difficulties of interpretation for an East German consumer.

## The 'relevance' approach to communication

The traditional view of communication has been to see it in terms of Saussurean linguistics and to describe the process as the simple transmission of messages, for example, Shannon and Weaver's 1949 model. Consequently, this has also been the approach taken to studying advertising communication. For example, the title of Judith Williamson's book *Decoding Advertisements* suggests that the advertiser is encoding the advertisements using his/her secret code which is unknown to the consumer and it is then up to the academic to break the code and reveal the advertisement's true and sinister message. However, this encoding-decoding approach is, in my opinion, unsuitable for describing the complexities of modern advertising and this is why I have chosen to design the model around relevance theory. Not only does the introduction of the concept of relevance overcome the problems associated with the *conduit* approach, it also provides a valid and worthwhile model for analysing inter-cultural advertising communication.

Central to the concept of relevance is the idea of context. By context, we mean the advertisee's total situation, which would include the individual, e.g. his/her personality, intelligence, interpersonal attitudes and beliefs. For obvious practical reasons, given that advertising is mass communication and thus cannot be tailor-made for the individual, these are not of concern in this investigation. Other factors which help to shape the advertisee's context would be economic considerations, such as income and purchasing power; his/her buying behaviour, for example, what is the advertisee's primary motive for buying, e. g. necessity or status, and also social factors, such as socio-economic status, education and lifestyle aspirations.

The total situation also encompasses the circumstances in which the advertisee encounters the advertisement, e. g. the channel in which the advertisement appears and the co-text surrounding the advertisement. In the context of the new federal states, East Germans tend to see the primary function of newspapers as that of providing information and editorial comment and are therefore very averse to meeting an advertisement – which they consider a waste of news space – in this context. The final and (from the point of view of this study) most important element in the advertisee's total situation or context is the advertisee's cultural knowledge, which I shall define as knowledge and experience obtained and reinforced by being part of a particular culture and society. The context which the advertisee chooses to interpret the advertisement will be determined by these factors. This also applies to the other participants in the advertising process. The advertiser and copywriter each have a particular situation or context which inevitably influences the production of the advertisement.

Successful communication therefore depends on the advertiser and advertisee using and choosing a common context. In order for the correct context to be chosen by the advertisee, the advertisement must be relevant to him/her, otherwise s/he will not waste valuable time and energy processing the information contained in it. Whether or not an advertisement is relevant will depend on whether it appeals to relevant needs and whether the advertisee has the cultural knowledge needed to interpret it.

## The model

Thus, we are presented with four possible situations and outcomes of inter-cultural advertising. In the first situation, the advertiser and advertisee share the same culture or sub-culture. As a result, they share – all things being equal – the same cultural knowledge, similar needs and other factors e.g. financial considerations. Obviously, this is an ideal situation which would seldom if ever exist in reality. Cultural knowledge, in the words of Sperber & Wilson, is 'infinitely regressive' and, as a result, the advertiser can make certain assumptions about the advertisee's cultural knowledge and needs because they share the same context. These assumptions are based on sets and sub-sets of assumptions which the advertiser doesn't even realise s/he is making, because when communicating with members of the same linguistic, economic, ideological and social culture, these are subconsciously taken for granted as being mutually known. For example, the advertiser would not think it necessary to tell the advertisee that this is an advertisement, since the advertisee should – by virtue of being a member of the same culture – be able to recognise an advertisement and to understand its function.

Much advertising today depends on the advertisee possessing vast quantities of cultural knowledge. For example, the advertisements for the Australian lager Castlemaine XXXX all play on the idea of four-letter-words. However, imagine the problems of interpretation for someone who did not know the significance of this symbol or a culture where taboo words didn't exist. Furthermore, many advertisements now build on cultural knowledge of other advertisements. For example, the recent television advertisements for Boddington's beer are a pun on the Cornetto ice-cream advertisements of a few years ago and depend on the advertisee having seen and remembering the Cornetto advertisements. Such tricks are necessary to attract the attention of sophisticated consumers, but are they appropriate in a less developed economy?

Sperber and Wilson maintain that the onus is on the speaker (in this case the advertiser) to decide what is and is not mutually known. When the advertiser fails to do this, the second situation occurs, where the advertiser is either unaware of, or ignores, the different culture or sub-culture of the advertisee. This was the initial situation faced by some West German advertisers when they used advertisements which had been designed and consumed in a mutual context in an attempt to address advertisees in a different culture.

Since culture, as defined in this model, constitutes the economic, ideological, social and linguistic framework of the advertiser and advertisee, it could be argued that it is impossible for the advertiser and advertisee to share the same needs and cultural knowledge, unless the advertiser is communicating with peers and fellow advertisers. However, broadly speaking, individuals within the same sub-culture or culture, region or country are more likely – all things being equal – to have the same cultural knowledge, economic situation etc. than individuals in different countries or regions.

In the third situation, the advertiser recognises that the advertisee has a different cultural context and that mutual knowledge may not exist. Thus, s/he adjusts the advertising message, but without sufficient reference to, or knowledge of the other culture. As a result, it will be very difficult for the advertisee to assign the correct context to the advertising message. There is an alternative interpretation of this situation based on the idea of multinational culture or McLuhan's notion of the global village. Transnational corporations, who actually inhabit this multinational limbo, design generic advertising in this multicultural context, with considerable success internationally.

The fourth situation provides the ideal outcome where the inter-cultural advertising communication is successful because the advertiser has produced the advertisement largely within the context of the advertisee. Therefore, the advertisee should be able to deal with the advertisement's cultural context using knowledge which s/he already has and the advertisement should also appeal to needs which are relevant to the advertisee. This kind of successful communication can be achieved by copywriters who either belong to or are very familiar with the particular culture and/or using market research tools effectively.

# Bank advertising

This study is being carried out using exclusively pre-*Wende* advertisements. The logic behind this is that, whether consciously or sub-consciously, advertisers and copywriters are now working within a different context, i. e. that of a unified Germany and we would expect that this would have affected the advertising they produce. Thus, from the point of view of testing the model, the most interesting thing is to take such pre-Wende advertisements and test them in the East German context.

I'd like to discuss an advertisement for Dresdner Bank within this framework. Cook (1992) talks about the increasing dominance of the paralinguistic element in advertisements today and the corresponding decrease in the amount of text used in advertisements. However this and all the other advertisements in this series contain huge amounts of text. In fact, it was the intention of Dresdner that this sober approach would enable the advertisements to take on the features (and perhaps the veracity??) of the surrounding co-text – in this case the business pages of the daily newspapers.

Before talking about the advertisement in detail and in order to understand what is and is not mutually known to advertiser and advertisee, we need to look at the banking context in the former GDR to see how it differed from western-style banking. First of all, although the GDR was very proud of its own version of socialism, the Soviet influence was still strong. The banking system was largely imported to East Germany as well as the other Eastern Bloc countries and the *Notenbank* (later the *Staatsbank*) was very much modelled on the Soviet *Gosbank*. It was therefore a completely dependent organ of the state, mainly concerned with the distribution of allocated funds. Another important factor to be taken into consideration is the traditionally negative view of banking in Marxist-Leninist thinking. As a result, the nationalisation of the banks was seen as essential in the process of setting up a socialist economy. Although this was 'the official line' and many private individuals may have thought differently, these attitudes permeated every aspect of public life in the former GDR and it would not be surprising if East Germans had an aversion to Western-style banking institutions.

Whilst economic units were obliged to bank with their local branch of the *Notenbank*, individuals banked with the *Sparkassen* or savings banks and credit-worthiness as it is understood in capitalist-style banking was largely unknown. Also, the *Staatsbank* exercised tight control over the economic efficiency of enterprises and was allowed to impose 'financial discipline' on erring units. Not surprisingly, the *Staatsbank* had an unpopular and inefficient image, its employees even being referred to as 'bureaucrats and parasites'. All of these factors have contributed to the East German definition of what a bank is and does and have helped to shape the total situation or context in which the advertisee in the new federal states views banks and advertisements for banks.

However, despite these differences, two important similarities between the old and new federal states should be kept in mind. First of all the Germans – both East and West – are very good savers and, secondly, the dominance of the savings and co-operative banks in providing services to individuals. With regard to the other side of the hypothesis, the needs appealed to in this particular advertisement are structured into a hierarchy based on Maslow's theory of needs. They range from quite basic needs such as the *need for security* and the *need to be prepared* to more obscure and 'sophisticated' needs such as the *need for status* and the *need for choice*. The needs towards the top of the pyramid are only relevant in a very advanced – in purely economic and consumerist terms – culture. In fact, many of them could be said to be manufactured needs, for example the *need for choice* and *flexibility*. Interestingly, the need to be managed tends to appear in much modern advertising. This is the (manufactured?) need to save time and hassle, by letting someone else take over some aspect of your life. Thus, whilst thinking you are independent and that you make independent and flexible choices, you are in fact surrendering much of your autonomy to a commercial enterprise to do with it as it sees fit.

Need to be managed
Need for flexibility
Need for choice
Need for status
Need to increase wealth
Need to invest
Need for assets/wealth
Need for logic
Need for information
Need to save
Need to have access to money
Need to be prepared
Need to have security
Need to hoard/accumulate

*The hierarchy of needs appealed to by advertisement*

Another interesting need appealed to is the *need for logic*, something which is perhaps a dominant feature of much German advertising. In this particular advertisement, this need is satisfied by making intangibles tangible. The theme of the advertisement is investing in gold, in something solid, rather than paper money which is too transient and intangible for the logical mind – even though the prospective investor is unlikely to return from Dresdner with a case full of ingots!! Furthermore, the advertisement talks about the bank investing customers' money in gold mines, thus tying everything together and leaving the advertisee in no doubt that this is a logical and sensible investment. One of the aims of the study is to discover whether or not these needs are relevant to the advertisees. We would expect that because the economy and consumer society in the former GDR were less developed than in the Federal Republic, the needs at the bottom of the pyramid (as far as the *need for assets*) would be more relevant to the East German consumer, particularly in this interim phase of transition. What advertisers have found to be most important in advertising in the new federal states is the *need for information*. This is hardly surprising, since, according to Pelster (1981), once specifically West German institutions are explained to the East German and vice versa, any communication problems should be solved.

This brings us to the other side of the hypothesis. What cultural knowledge is needed to interpret the advertisement? In other words, what elements of the advertisement are *redundant* (a term used by Shannon and Weaver), as opposed to entropic or new and unexpected? We need to ask what does the advertiser assume is mutually known? Starting with the most basic assumptions, we can say that the advertiser assumes that the advertisee is able to recognise that this is an advertisement, that s/he knows who the advertisement is for and what its function is. In the East German context, this would include the ability to differentiate advertising from propaganda. Since consumers in the former GDR were used to such straightforward slogans as *Plaste und Elaste aus Schkopau*, it may not be quite so easy for them to understand that a highly sophisticated, subliminal and atmospheric advertisement with little information is trying to achieve the same end. Another basic assumption made by the advertiser is that the advertisee knows that this is an advertisement for a bank and that Dresdner is a bank in the sense that the advertiser understands the functions and definition of such an institution. This is where the residual East German banking context may have an effect on the interpretation of the advertisement.

The advertisement is based around gold and makes many assumptions about the advertisee's positive attitude towards gold as a symbol of safety and security. This notion of securing the value of money runs deep in West Germans, given the past experience of hyperinflation and a worthless currency. However, is this as important to the East Germans – particularly those born and brought up in the former GDR. Furthermore, the advertisement takes for granted that the advertisee considers old things to be valuable. However, it is only in very developed and affluent societies that antiques are collected and antiquities valued. Therefore, is this assumption valid in the new federal states? In many post-communist countries, including East Germany, there has been a great demand for new things and a break with the past.

The advertisement also assumes that the advertisee views risk-taking negatively and thus wishes to avoid risk, whereas saving and planning are assumed to be positively viewed. However, the North American attitude to what is and is not a risk would be very different to the conservative German attitude. Likewise, it is taken for granted that the advertisee sees responsible speculating as acceptable. But does this also apply to the new federal states, considering that any form of speculation would have been frowned upon by the former GDR regime?

Dresdner Bank did not use these advertisements in the new federal states. Instead it has concentrated on an information-oriented campaign explaining the features of Western-style banking. Dresdner is also the bank with the highest recognition rate in the new federal states, which is hardly surprising given the 'homecoming' theme of much of its marketing, exploiting the bank's origins in the city of Dresden, and its high public profile e. g. the sponsoring of buses for the city of Dresden. What is of interest in this study is not Dresdner Bank's campaign in the new federal states, but rather why these or similar advertisements were not used. Further research is intended to show that this is because the needs appealed to in these advertisements are not relevant to the advertisee and that the advertisee does not have the cultural knowledge needed to interpret them.

# References

Cook, G. (1992) *The Discourse of Advertising*. London: Routledge.

Deckers, J. (1974) *Die Transformation des Bankensystems in der Sowjetischen Besatzungszone/DDR*. Berlin: Verlag Duncker u. Humboldt.

Fowles, J. (1990) Advertising's fifteen basic appeals. In P. Escholz, A. Rosa and V. Clark (eds) *Language Awareness*. New York: St. Martin's Press Inc.

Hannan, Brian. (1990) Making the most of East Germany's media changes. *Business Marketing Digest (UK)* 15/2, 131-137.

Humphreys, G. (1990) Bridging the East-West Divide. *Euromoney* March 1990, 73-82.

Leiss, W. , Kline, S. and Jhally, S. (1990) *Social Communication in Advertising*. London: Routledge.

Sperber, D. and Wilson, D. (1986) *Relevance: Communication and cognition*. Oxford: Basil Blackwell.

Stehling, H. (1992) Wir treten im Finanzmarkt als Alleswisser auf. *Horizont* 1/2, 1992, p. 14.

Vestergaard, T. and Schroder, K. (1985) *The Language of Advertising.* Oxford: Basil Blackwell.
Williamson, J. (1978) *Decoding Advertisements: Ideology and meaning in advertisements.* London: Marion Boyars.
Zimmermann, H. et al (1985) *DDR Handbuch.* Cologne: Verlag Wissenschaft und Politik.
Einfach lächerlich. *Der Spiegel* 22/1990, 114-115.
The Problems of Unity. *Euromoney* September 1990, Special supplement p.11.
Various Dresdner Bank AG internal publications.

# 7 'I thought I could write until I came here': Student writing in higher education

MARY LEA
*University of North London*

## Introduction

Today's students in higher education are frequently perceived by their tutors as having difficulties with writing; these difficulties are often considered as being due to the students' lack of knowledge of grammar and syntax. Writing problems are particularly acute with respect to mature students and those from non-traditional educational backgrounds. Research carried out with a group of students from one of the new London universities suggests that to understand what is happening in student writing it is necessary to examine different frameworks, and the ways in which these interact in students' written assignments. The approach of this paper is to consider writing practices within their social context and takes account of various influences on students' writing practices: past and present, both within and outside the university. Difficulties with writing are not regarded as issues to be dealt with by study skills and learning support specialists outside subject areas.

## Background to the research

The research has been carried out amongst university undergraduates, many of whom are mature students from non-traditional, educational backgrounds. Students have self selected to attend a 'Writing and Language Centre' in order to consider their own problem areas of writing and language use in higher education. During consultation with a writing researcher, students work on their own written assignments to tackle the difficulties that both they and their tutors experience with their written work. The research has considered writing practices in terms of three perspectives:

 *students' written assignments;*
 *students' self commentaries on their own writing;*
 *staff comments on marked assignments.*

64

Graddol, D and Thomas, S. (1994)
*Language in a Changing Europe,*
Clevedon: BAAL and Multilingual Matters

The rationale behind the project has been to develop a methodology which will enable both staff and students to develop a clearer understanding of the processes that are at work when students are writing in an academic environment.

## Social context

Various authors have referred to the importance of social context in the consideration of literacy and linguistic practices. Street (1984) suggests that literacy practices are not autonomous and are related to specific cultural contexts, which themselves are associated with relations of power and ideology. Ballard and Clancy consider context in respect of academic literacy and suggest that 'becoming literate involves becoming acculturated: learning to read and write the culture'. They pay particular attention to the function of language within the university culture and define literacy as 'a student's capacity to use written language to perform those functions required by the culture in ways and at a level judged acceptable by the reader' (1988:8). Sheeran and Barnes, with reference to school literacy, talk about the academic 'ground rules' which pupils need to identify within any one subject and the fact that such 'ground rules' are frequently ' unclear, changeable, and open to interpretation' (1991:1). In relation to linguistic practices, Fairclough (1989) suggests that any examination of texts needs to consider the relationship between texts, the processes of their production and interpretation and the social conditions of their production and interpretation. Following from these authors, it would seem that any useful analysis of student writing would necessarily have to take account of the social context in which it had been produced.

When considering academic writing practices within the social context of an institute of higher education, I would like to suggest that it is possible to identify four different frameworks within which we can examine student writing; at any point in time there seems to be a permanent process of interplay between these frameworks. The frameworks can be identified as follows:

*language structure and form;*

*features of subject specific discourses;*

*an academic discourse of an ideological nature;*

*students' other language experiences.*

## Language structure and form

This is the traditional category that most staff and students refer to when they express concern about writing. Staff frequently make reference to students' difficulties with grammar, syntax and punctuation; students themselves suggest that if they had a more efficient grasp of some of these concepts they would be more effective writers:

> I haven't got a knowledge of grammar that I think maybe I should have. I have been sitting down and thinking this is what I want to say. How do I say it?

> ....And trying out different sentences. It drives me mad but I think it's probably a good thing to do. And try to play around with say short sentences and long sentences and try to make it a bit more interesting and things.

> Well I mean I find it hard to know what a verb is and I keep promising myself..I've got one of those grammar books and I'll sit there and learn it all but I never have the time.

> My sentences are inclined to be very long, they're long because I'm not sure where commas and that should be going.

These comments came from students who strongly believed that their writing could be enhanced by the application of a better knowledge of grammar in their assignments. Comments by academic staff about a student's lack of knowledge of grammar are frequently coupled with comments about an inability to structure written work appropriately.

> Use of language skills need to be developed. Arguments are sometimes rendered ineffective because of weaknesses in this area.

> You must make sure that any quotations fit in syntactically.

> You are being held back by a lack of care and thought in relation to your grammar, spelling and overall essay construction. In terms of your sentence construction you need to be careful about your use of words for expressing your ideas. Your essay structure starts off well but about half way through it starts to read like a shopping list of points and we have no conclusion.

> There were a fair number of spelling and grammatical errors, as well as some repetitions of points, and I suggest that you might do some work on your writing style.

The difficulty with such comments is that they give students no explicit knowledge as to how to acquire the skills that are being alluded to or even what these skills are.

# Features of subject specific, academic discourses

Each discipline and each subject within each discipline have specific ways of ordering and presenting knowledge. What is regarded as appropriate in one subject may be regarded as inappropriate in another. Bazerman (1981) suggests that the way in which language is used in different academic contexts creates different assumptions about the body of knowledge that the writer and reader shares, and this creates contrasting methods of representing information in academic discourses. Peter Elbow (1991) has outlined the very disparate nature of the different discourses within English studies alone: the contrast between the rhetorical tradition of C.S. Lewis with today's psychoanalytic theorists and these two with post structuralist, continental discourse. Susan Peck Mc Donald (1991) has identified the lengthy nominal style of literary critics in academic literary writing and the use of non-standardised terminology and referentially vague terms. Students' commentaries on their own writing frequently make reference to difficulty with vocabulary and terminology; yet in order to become a successful writer in the university the student has to incorporate these features of subject specific discourses into her own writing:

> I don't think that I can say things in a more complicated way until I've got the terminology.

> That's one thing I'm trying to do as well....like to increase my vocabulary. but then spelling is so difficult.

> One can know lots of new words and then not know how to spell them and I think that's a problem with being self educated as well, which I think I am in a sense.For me you often read new words and you don't have the faintest idea how to say them.

> There are quite a lot of words in the English course, for instance semiotics, deixis, which I haven't come across before and have difficulty understanding what they mean.

> I wasn't sure whether I was required to write about the structure of the actual poem.

At the same time, emulating academic discourses can result in an incomprehensible written style as students try to negotiate this new language:

> Franco's regime had been able to formulate a language to produce a total mentality which seemingly conditioned the minds of his country men with one ideological homogeneous conglomerate and thus successfully repressing the spirit of Spain for four decades.

Additionally tutors' comments frequently refer to an inappropriacy of language use within a particular discourse and may make elusive reference to the way in which written work is expected to be organised within a discipline:

> You've done a lot of work on this and I'm glad to see an appropriate bibliography. However you have not linked the first part of the question to the second. As I told you after your seminar the first part of the question is theoretical, to be answered with reference to Kuznets, summarized by Ghatak and Ingersent, as I presented them in class.

> I think this assignment faces problems of form and content, as well as language.In terms of form, it is closer to an essay rather than a Ist assignment format.e.g. your lengthy discussion of the Law and Order sequence could have benefited from the use of a shot analysis. In terms of content, you didn't always draw out the differences between the two extracts.e.g. you initially failed to mention the narrator and then said there was one in a later comment..Finally your sentence structure and grammar is shaky.

## An academic discourse of an ideological nature

The third framework may be considered as a super-ordinate category which in some senses embraces the other categories. Following from Fairclough (1989), I have suggested that any examination of student writing should take account of the context of the text's production: students within the university write for their tutors. Their writing reflects the students' understanding of what is required of them and this interpretation to a large part will be conditioned by feedback on previous written assignments. Unfortunately academic conventions generally remain implicit and students have difficulty accessing what is required from the tutors' feedback. In addition to trying to understand features of subject specific discourses, students seem to be trying to access some ideological notion of what is required in their writing through an interpretation of the tutors' comments. Fairclough (1992) writing on ideology helps an understanding of how these implicit conventions become embedded as the 'common sense' way of writing assignments:

> I shall understand ideologies to be significations/constructions of reality (the physical world, social relations, social identities), which are built into various dimensions of the forms/meanings of discursive practises....The ideologies embedded in discursive practices are most effective when they become naturalized, and achieve the status of common sense. (Fairclough,1992:87)

Although students are able to access particular features of subject specific discourse they still seem to be trying to grasp some other notion of what is, and what is not, acceptable or appropriate in their writing at the University and their comments frequently allude to this ideological notion:

> .....that's probably what I need to focus on. Having more of an argument maybe as well, because I often find it easy to write an essay if you've got a definite point of view that you really want to put across. There are wording of essays that open themselves to that and I often find it easier if I've got a definite point of view that I can swing everything around.

> Another important point is finding out what the tutor wants, like for some tutors they would allow that, some tutors are very hung up about the narrator and the narrator is never the author, and other tutors say that's not like a bug of theirs.

> I don't really know, is one allowed to say that?

> Whereas for example, some tutors are quite happy for you to use 'I' whereas others I think maybe still wouldn't be. I wouldn't like to use 'I' because it's been drilled into me that you don't unless they say you can, I think on my Access course. You'd never use 'I', you'd never be that personal and it annoys me because it would be a lot more helpful often to use 'I' and you read a lot of books, critics and they always seem to use 'I'

> I feel I have to write the way the tutor wants me to write.

Tutors' comments on students' written work also seem to echo this ideological notion of appropriacy:

> Try to use quotes to back up your argument.

> Could you develop this?

> You need to back this up more firmly.

> This seems like an added point but you haven't really argued this.

> Your grasp of Bazin's general argument is good and your criticisms well made. This is at a conceptual level, but you textual analysis doesn't quite drive home the points you have raised, usually falling short of explaining how such and such a feature does not fit with Bazin's idea.

> Why? You need to put this into context.

> Have you argued this?

Such comments make reference to developing particular ways of ordering written knowledge without any explicit reference as to how students are meant to accomplish this. To be able to understand how to develop an argument, create structure, or 'drive home points' students need a clearer understanding of the processes that are involved and the ways that these are manifest in writing. The tutors' comments give no indication of this but make allusion to some ideological notion of academic discourse, the 'common sense' way of presenting written knowledge in higher education.

## Students' other language experiences.

The final framework concerns other language experiences, other discourses within which the student participates, features of which may contrast, compete and conflict with discourses within the environment of higher education, In matters of language form tutors may be inclined to identify the influence of dialect in writing as being ungrammatical, and have difficulties identifying influences from more commonly used spoken language forms. A student struggling with an unfamiliar subject area may have problems finding the most appropriate register and she may slide into a 'journalese' which contains some elements of the formal style that she is trying to emulate. She may be aware that previous language experiences do not equip her for the requirements of higher education but she still has difficulty making the transition from one discourse to another:

> It's like learning a different language here. I speak differently than I do at home. It is a new language that you use here. It's something that has to be learnt. It is a tool that has to be learnt. You're using words like didactic and when you are outside it doesn't mean anything.

> You have to write about things in a different way. For example, in film I've always just seen a film and had particular reactions but now I have to write about it in a particular way and I can't see it that way. It's as if all the ways I've used before don't seem to matter here.

> I think it's with working twenty odd years in industry and that.....it needs to get things done by the end of the day so therefore you can have one point and then you can jump to number five but you can always come back to number two ... but it doesn't work like that in academic writing.

Students seem to find it difficult to draw on previous experiences of language use and incorporate them into their writing practices at the University. They frequently conceptualise previous skills as being inappropriate – or even invalid – in the present context but cannot find new ways of filling the gap. The comments on their written work may also imply inappropriacy but students are probably already aware of the contrasts between these academic discourses and those more familiar to them. Feedback does not give explicit direction as to how to move from one discourse to another:

Avoid this kind of journalistic non-sentence.

You are clearly longing to slide off into a psychoanalytic analysis of film - but are right to resist it! It's not appropriate to the question in hand, or to the word limit imposed.

In certain cases you need to be careful about your use of words for expressing your ideas.

## Conclusion

Identifying these four different frameworks,and considering the social context in which students are writing, should give us a clearer picture of the difficulties that students are facing when they begin to write in higher education for the first time. If difficulties with writing are perceived by academic staff as existing within only one framework: language structure and form, independently of all other, then students will have difficulty benefiting from their tutors' comments on their written assignments. It is useful for staff to be able to see that, for example, apparent grammatical problems cannot be considered outside an understanding of the overuse of terminology within a particular discipline. In the same way the inability to structure written work effectively may be a process of interplay between students' ideological notions of academic discourse and influences from other more dominant discourses.

Using these frameworks may enable us to understand how constraining writing in higher education can appear to students, and consider the processes that would have to be set in place in order to make writing practices more explicit. Work in critical linguistics, carried out at Lancaster University by Clark and Ivanic (1991), would suggest that students can be helped to understand their own practices as writers in higher education through the development of a critical language awareness.

A corollary to this approach with students could be the explicit identification by academic staff of the ways in which knowledge is expected to be ordered and processed in the written form within their own subject areas. It seems clear that the gap between students' and staff expectations needs to be closed; looking at writing practices in context on this multi-dimensional level and considering the influences of the different frameworks, should hopefully go some way towards closing the gap between staff and student perceptions of writing in higher education.

# References

Ballard, B. & Clanchy, J. (1988) Literacy in the university: An anthropological approach. In R. Gordon et al (eds) *Literacy by Degrees*. Milton Keynes: Open University Press.

Bazerman, C. (1981) What written knowledge does: three examples of academic discourse. *Philosophy of the Social Sciences*,11, 361-87.

Clark, R.& Ivanic, R. (1991) Consciousness-raising about the writing process. In

James, C. & Garrett, P. eds. *Language Awareness in the Classroom*. London: Longman.

Elbow, P. (1991) Reflections on Academic Discourse: How it relates to freshman and Colleagues. *College English*, Volume 53. Number 2.

Fairclough, N. (1989) *Language and Power*. London: Longman.

Fairclough, N. (1992) *Discourse and Social Change*. Cambridge: Polity.

Peck Mac Donald, S. (1990) The literary argument and its discursive conventions. In Nash, W. *The Writing Scholar*. Newbury Park: Sage.

Sheeran, Y. & Barnes, D. (1991) *School writing: Discovering the ground rules*. Milton Keynes: Open University Press.

Street, B.V. (1984) *Literacy in Theory and Practice*. Cambridge: Cambridge University Press.

# 8 Peer Observation and Post-lesson Discussion

BRIAN PARKINSON AND SHEENA DAVIES
*University of Edinburgh*

## Introduction

Anyone who is interested in using classroom observation for research and/or teacher development has to come to terms with a paradox or conflict. On the one hand, it seems that observing classes is essential if we are to understand what goes on. Questionnaires, interviews, diaries etc. can be useful, but anyone who regularly sits at the back of classes knows that what teachers and learners say about their lessons, what they believe about their lessons, is at best a very partial truth. On the other hand, there is widespread fear and mistrust of the outsider, whether researcher or teacher educator or both, coming into the classroom, and at the end of projects, however well intentioned, teachers may feel that they have been 'used', that the outsiders have followed their own agenda, that teachers have been misled and misunderstood and have derived little or no benefit from the exercise.

This paper reports on a project, intended to function as research and as teacher development, which tried to resolve this conflict by providing teachers with opportunities to observe each other, using a recognised lesson coding scheme, and to discuss the lessons afterwards. The researchers attended neither the lessons nor the discussion, but the latter were recorded and used as the basis for the research report.

We see our research as broadly within the tradition of Fanselow (1977), who recommended systematic classroom observation for 'generating and exploring alternatives', and also in line with the recent interest in cooperative development (e.g. Lockhart, 1991; Edge, 1992; Underhill, 1992). It is, however, unique as far as we know in its use of systematic coding systems, alongside less structured analysis, at two stages – by the teachers in analysing each other's lessons, and by the researchers (using a completely different system) in analysing the discussions.

Graddol, D and Thomas, S. (1994)
*Language in a Changing Europe,*
Clevedon: BAAL and Multilingual Matters

# The Context of our Research

The research took place in 1992 on General English classes at the Institute for Applied Language Studies, University of Edinburgh. The General English course is a full-time course of 20 hours per week and the students are, in the main, young adults of various nationalities who come for a full term of 11 weeks. The majority study English to improve employment opportunities, a minority to prepare for post-graduate qualifications. Classes at different times of the day focus on the development of different skills.

The teachers are all well-qualified professionals, and all had had previous experience of being observed and observing others. Three had briefly encountered coding systems some years earlier on a master's course in applied linguistics; beyond this, however, none had ever used particular coding systems, and no structured system of peer observation has, to date, been set up at IALS.

# The Experiment

## Objectives

These were stated as follows in the research proposal:

1      To provide teachers with an opportunity to learn by observing other teachers' lessons, receiving comments on their own and discussing issues arising, supported if required by classroom observation literature (Allwright & Bailey etc).

2      To inform the academic community on the outcome of this process (research paper) with particular attention to:

     (i)   the terms in which teachers conceptualise their own and others' lessons
     (ii)  what is perceived as different
     (iii) what is perceived as surprising
     (iv)  what attracts positive, negative and neutral comment
     (v)   what use, if any, is made of classroom observation instruments or other help provided (vi) in what ways, if at all, teachers would like to continue the peer education and self- education process.

## General Procedure

Eight teachers – all those working on the GE course at the time – were invited to participate in the project, on a voluntary basis, and all agreed. They were put into four pairs, and each member of the pair observed one lesson by the other member for at least one hour (lessons last 90 or 100 minutes). The teachers then had a post-lesson discussion in two parts, one for each lesson, each part to last approximately 30 minutes. The researchers were not present at either lessons or discussion, except in one case where a researcher (SD) was one of the teachers. The lessons were not recorded but the discussions were, and the research was conducted on the understanding that discussions, not lessons, were the main focus of investigation. It was also stressed that the research was non-evaluative in a double sense: observers should not 'judge' the lessons, and researchers would not judge the discussion comments: the purpose was mainly one of professional development exploring whatever issues were of interest.

Tapes of the discussions were transcribed (by research assistants who were experienced EFL teachers), and these transcripts (checked with the original where necessary) constitute the main part of our data. They were supplemented by two minor data sources, not discussed in the paper:

(i)    the completed coding sheets used by the observers

(ii)   a post-discussion questionnaire

The teacher/observers were given a selection of recognised coding systems, with background information (see below), and asked to select one of these before observing and use it during observation. In addition, they were asked to make notes of anything observed which was not covered by the system but which seemed surprising, interesting, etc. (cf. research questions, of which observers had a copy). To facilitate this, observers were provided with a three-page coding sheet with space for both system-based comments and open-ended comments.

The observers were not expected to use the systems 'properly', i.e. to make exhaustive coding using exact definitions. This would have been impossible without extensive training. Instead, they were asked to use them as a basis for entries which indicated the main patterns of the lesson. It was stressed, however, that something more than a general impression was required, and that sequential, timed coding should be attempted.

In the post-lesson discussion the teacher/observers were asked to discuss the lessons in whatever way they felt useful. This could be, but did not have to be, based partly on the coding sheets.

### Lesson coding systems offered and used

A choice of 8 published lesson coding systems was offered, and 3 actually used by one or more observers. These were the BIAS system (Brown 1975), the Bowers system (Bowers 1980) and the COLT system (Fröhlich et al. 1985).

## Data analysis

This comprised several elements, both quantitative and qualitative, only one of which is reported here: for this, we devised a two-dimensional coding system, covering (i) the types of topics discussed and (ii) the ways in which teachers interacted, and what we perceived as the underlying speech acts. Our categories were largely 'post-hoc', i.e. created to cover what we found in the transcripts, but we attempted to keep in mind our research questions and make only those distinctions necessary to answer these. The system was devised jointly by both researchers, and several joint codings were attempted in order first to improve and then to measure inter-coder reliability.

| Number | Topic | Example |
|--------|-------|---------|
| 1 | Facts about students e.g. nationality, level, age, 'history' | "He's been here for ages and he's going to be here for even further ages" |
| 2 | Observation system used by coder | "That's the, em the one that is supposed to measure the social functions of the language that goes on" |
| 3 | Expectations | "Had you got any preconceived ideas about what would be happening?" |
| 4 | Relation between expectations and events | "No well I suppose I imagined probably about what I saw, I mean some input and some practice and some real communication". |
| 5 | The observed lesson (general) | "So that's why they had this sort of check-list they were using." |
| 5.1 | The observed lesson (learner behaviour) | "He was making a face [...] he wasn't seeking confirmation". |
| 5.2 | The observed lesson (teacher behaviour) | "And at one point you sort of broke off everything and said 'You look puzzled' ". |
| 6 | Other lessons by same teacher (general) | "We had been doing quite a lot of work beforehand on discussion techniques". |
| 6.1 | Other lessons by same teacher (learner behaviour) | "He doesn't often do that actually" |
| 6.2 | Other lessons by same teacher (teacher behaviour) | "In that kind of situation I don't, er, if they ask me a question I just turn away". |
| 7 | Other lessons by observer (general) | Similar to 5 and 6 |
| 7.1 | Other lessons by observer (learner behaviour) | Similar to 5.1 and 6.2. |
| 7.2 | Other lessons by observer (teacher behaviour) | Similar to 5.2 and 6.2. |
| 8 | Other lessons or lessons in general (general) | Similar to 5 and 6 |
| 8.1 | Other lessons or lessons in general (learner behaviour) | Similar to 5.1 and 6.1. |
| 8.2 | Other lessons or lessons in general (teacher behaviour) | Similar to 5.2 and 6.2. |
| 9 | Linguistic theories/concepts | "It's amazing how much, well er, I won't say students, I mean anyone can, how much you can read without actually taking any of it in." |
| 10 | Materials and syllabus | "Was that something that came up in the textbook?" |
| 11.1 | Personal feelings (general) | "I was genuinely surprised" |
| 11.2 | Feelings about being observed | "... when you've sort of er being watched by your peers as it were, you do feel a certain, that you are being judged [...] it is a bit nerve-racking..." |
| 11.3 | Feelings about discussing lesson | "I don't want to sort of make any evaluative commennts or judgments on the thing |

| 12 | The English language | "But I mean what is the actual dictionary definition of 'authoritative'?" |
| 13.1 | The project in general | "Well it seems to me that to get the most value from anything like this, viewing each other once is just nothing like enough." |
| 13.2 | Observation in general | "I wonder how far what one learns from observing is actually useful when you're actually teaching. Maybe it is in the planning stage." |
| 14 | Other | What did you say? |

| Label | "Speech Acts" | Examples |
|---|---|---|
| BC | Back-channelling | "Ah, I see. Right, right." |
| SY | Sympathising | "This is a big problem isn't it, that everybody has." |
| SP | Speculating | "Maybe she only talked a lot the second time because she was [playing another role]. " |
| QN | Question (neutral) | "Was it difficult to try to use it?" |
| QC | Question (challenge) | "But why did me being there stop you doing it spontaneou[sly]?" |
| INF | Informing | "After you left they started discussing again." |
| OP | Opinionating | "I think X is very much a sort of actor anyway." |
| EV+ | Evaluation (positive) | "It was good that it was slipping into real discussion." |
| EV- | Evaluation (negative) | (i) "[My] board work was pretty awful" (ii) "The only thing was, the only thing was, that it was, they, the particular constructions with the particular prompts did seem to be causing some rather odd constructions..." |
| IE | Inviting evaluation | "Was there anything else that surprised you, that you wanted to ask me why you did something? 'Cos it's very useful for me as well to get sort of, a reaction of some kind." |
| A | Adverting or semi-phatic | "You reminded them about erm what they had done the previous,week." |
| J | Justifying | "I mean the point of that exercise was to see whether they had actually got their heads round the, em, the distinction." |
| SG | Suggesting | "If they'd had a piece of paper with it written down it probably would have been easier." |
| AG | Agreeing | "Yes, Anna said that a couple of times, yes." |
| Other | Other | "Oh, maybe." |

N.B. These 'speech acts' must be interpreted in their interaction with different topic categories, and with who (teacher or observer) is speaking. For example, commonsense suggests that evaluating one's own lesson, one's interlocutor's lesson and a third party's lesson are three very different kinds of speech acts. The grand total for each 'speech act' may thus sometimes be less illuminating than totals for individual combinations of topic and 'speech act'.

# Results

Our full report contains tables showing the pattern of interaction in all 8 post-lesson discussions. Space permits the inclusion here only of two aggregate tables (though findings on individual interviews are mentioned in the later discussion). These tables show overall use by teachers and observers respectively of the various topics, speech acts and combinations of these. 'Teacher' and 'observer' of course refer to the role taken in the lesson preceding the discussion: all eight participants took both roles, but in different lessons.

Table 1

Observer Moves - Grand Total

| | | BC | SY | SP | QN | QC | INF | OP | EV+ | EV- | IE | A | CN | J | SG | AG | Other | Total |
|---|---|---|---|---|---|---|---|---|---|---|---|---|---|---|---|---|---|---|
| 1 | Facts about students | 6 | 2 | 1 | 15 | 4 | 1 | 3 | | | | 3 | | | | 2 | | 37 |
| 2 | Coding system | 2 | | | 1 | | 38 | 4 | 1 | 11 | | | | 1 | | | 1 | 59 |
| 3 | Expectations | | | 1 | | | 4 | | | 1 | | | | | | | | 6 |
| 4 | Relation expect/event | | | 1 | 1 | | 5 | | | 1 | | 1 | | | | | | 9 |
| 5 | Observed lesson (general) | 22 | 5 | 3 | 9 | 2 | 21 | 5 | 28 | 6 | 1 | 16 | 2 | 1 | 3 | 1 | 2 | 127 |
| 5.1 | Observed lesson (SS) | 7 | 1 | 5 | 7 | 4 | 28 | 26 | 23 | 7 | | 37 | | 5 | 2 | 12 | | 164 |
| 5.2 | Observed lesson (T) | 1 | 2 | | 8 | 5 | 17 | 9 | 37 | 10 | | 31 | | 9 | 6 | 1 | | 136 |
| 6 | T's lesson (general) | 10 | | | 9 | 4 | 2 | 2 | | | | | | | | | | 27 |
| 6.1 | T's lesson (SS) | 7 | | 1 | 5 | | | 1 | | | | | | | | | | 14 |
| 6.2 | T's lesson (T) | 3 | 1 | | 8 | | | 3 | | | | | | 1 | | | | 16 |
| 7 | O's lesson (general) | | 1 | | 2 | | 12 | | | | | | | | 1 | | | 16 |
| 7.1 | O's lesson (SS) | | | | | | 1 | | | | | | | | | | | 1 |
| 7.2 | O's lesson (T) | | | | | | 4 | | | | | | | | | | | 4 |
| 8 | Other lessons (gen.) | 2 | 7 | 1 | 3 | | 6 | 5 | | | | 1 | | | 1 | 3 | | 29 |
| 8.1 | Other lessons (SS) | 2 | | 1 | | | 3 | 8 | | | | 1 | | | | 3 | | 18 |
| 8.2 | Other lessons (T) | 3 | 1 | 2 | | | 3 | 3 | | | | | | | 1 | | | 13 |
| 9 | Theory | | | 2 | | | 4 | 6 | | | | | | | | | | 12 |
| 10 | Material | 6 | | 1 | 9 | 2 | | 1 | 1 | | | 3 | | | | | | 23 |
| 11.1 | Feelings (general) | 1 | | | 1 | | 10 | | | | | | | | | | | 12 |
| 11.2 | Feelings (observed) | | | 4 | 2 | | 5 | 7 | | | | | 1 | | | 2 | | 21 |
| 11.3 | Feelings (discussing) | | | | | | 5 | | | 1 | | | | | | | | 6 |
| 12 | English | 2 | | 1 | 4 | 1 | 3 | 1 | | | | 1 | 1 | | | 1 | | 15 |
| 13 | Project/obs. (general) | | | 1 | | | 1 | 4 | | | | | | | | | | 6 |
| 14 | Other | | | 2 | | | 1 | | | | | | | | 1 | | 2 | 6 |
| | TOTAL | 74 | 20 | 23 | 87 | 23 | 174 | 88 | 90 | 37 | 1 | 94 | 4 | 17 | 14 | 26 | 5 | 777 |

Table 2

Teacher Moves - Grand Total

| | | BC | SY | SP | QN | QC | INF | OP | EV+ | EV- | IE | A | CN | J | SG | AG | Other | Total |
|---|---|---|---|---|---|---|---|---|---|---|---|---|---|---|---|---|---|---|
| 1 | Facts about students | 2 | | | | | 35 | 4 | 2 | | | 1 | | | | 4 | | 48 |
| 2 | Coding system | 6 | | 1 | 6 | 1 | 3 | | | | 1 | 2 | 2 | 1 | | 1 | | 24 |
| 3 | Expectations | | | | 2 | 1 | | | | | | | | | | | | 3 |
| 4 | Relation expect/event | | | | 2 | | 9 | | | 1 | 1 | | | | | | | 13 |
| 5 | Observed lesson (general) | 16 | | | 6 | | 28 | 9 | 8 | 4 | 8 | 16 | 3 | 31 | | 8 | 1 | 138 |
| 5.1 | Observed lesson (SS) | 3 | 1 | 4 | 5 | | 29 | 20 | 13 | 5 | 1 | 17 | | 6 | | 11 | 1 | 116 |
| 5.2 | Observed lesson (T) | 10 | | 3 | 2 | | 7 | 1 | 6 | 4 | 9 | 4 | 9 | 33 | 3 | | 1 | 92 |
| 6 | T's lesson (general) | 1 | | | 1 | | 35 | 5 | | 1 | 1 | | 1 | 3 | | 2 | | 50 |
| 6.1 | T's lesson (SS) | | | 1 | 1 | | 42 | 11 | 3 | 3 | | 1 | | 1 | | | | 63 |
| 6.2 | T's lesson (T) | | | | | | 35 | | 1 | | 1 | 1 | | 14 | | 1 | | 53 |
| 7 | O's lesson (general) | | | | | | 2 | | | | | 1 | | | | | | 3 |
| 7.1 | O's lesson (SS) | | | | | | | | | | | | | | | | | 0 |
| 7.2 | O's lesson (T) | | | | | | | | | | | | | | | | | 0 |
| 8 | Other lessons (gen.) | 2 | | 1 | | | 2 | 8 | | | 1 | 2 | | 1 | | 3 | | 20 |
| 8.1 | Other lessons (SS) | 1 | 1 | | | | 3 | 9 | 1 | 2 | | 1 | | | | 3 | | 21 |
| 8.2 | Other lessons (T) | | | 2 | | | 3 | 7 | | | | | 1 | | 1 | | | 14 |
| 9 | Theory | 1 | | 1 | | | 2 | 5 | | | | | | | | 1 | | 9 |
| 10 | Material | 1 | | 1 | | | 18 | 1 | 1 | 2 | | 2 | 2 | 1 | | | | 29 |
| 11.1 | Feelings (general) | | | 1 | 1 | 1 | 6 | 1 | | | | | | 1 | | | | 11 |
| 11.2 | Feelings (observed) | 2 | | 4 | | 4 | 4 | 4 | | | | | | | | 2 | | 20 |
| 11.3 | Feelings (discussing) | | | | | | | | | | | | | | | | | 0 |
| 12 | English | 1 | 1 | 1 | 1 | | 2 | 3 | | | | | | | | 1 | | 10 |
| 13 | Project/obs. (general) | | | | | | 1 | 2 | | | | | | | | | | 3 |
| 14 | Other | 1 | | | 3 | | 4 | 1 | | | | | | | | 1 | | 10 |
| | TOTAL | 47 | 3 | 19 | 30 | 5 | 269 | 94 | 36 | 22 | 22 | 47 | 20 | 91 | 4 | 38 | 3 | 750 |

Randomly selected samples of the data were coded by both researchers to yield inter-coder reliability figures. Agreement on segmentation was only 74%, due mainly to different treatment of brief asides and backchannelling, but this did not seem to distort the overall picture. Agreement on topic was 85%, but on 'speech acts' it was only 66%.

# Discussion and Conclusions

## The transcript codings: 'topic' dimension

The following general features may be noted:

(i)    In all discussions for both speakers the observed lesson (category 5, including 5.1 and 5.2) is, not surprisingly, the main topic.

(ii)   Within this category the emphasis varies, some discussions emphasising learner behaviour, some teacher behaviour, some more evenly balanced. On the whole, however, learners were discussed more than teachers. This may reflect both the current climate of opinion within EFL and the perceived usefulness of another perspective on learner interaction.

(iii)  The second most consistently frequent category – more than 10 codings in each of six discussions – was category 6 (including 6.1 and 6.2), i.e. what the observed teacher did in other lessons, including parts of the observed lesson before and after observation. The felt need to put observed events in context is unsurprising.

(iv)   The only other categories which even approached this frequency – each having more than 10 codings in each of four discussions – were category 8 (including 8.1 and 8.2), i.e. lessons in general, and category 2, the coding system.

(v)    Only three other categories ever exceeded the '10 codings' threshold, and these only in one discussion each, reflecting a particular focus of that discussion. These were:

    The teaching material (category 10) in discussion 2B

    Feelings about being observed (category 11.2) in discussion 2A

    The English language (category 12) in discussion 1B

(vi)   There was a tendency for similar topics to be discussed in each of a pair of discussions with the same participants (i.e. 1A and 1B, 2A and 2B etc.).

At this point it may be worth repeating that the ethos of the project was non-evaluative, and we shall not presume to suggest that high or low use of any topic is 'good' or 'bad'. The teachers discussed what they identified as worth discussing, exactly as intended.

If one were planning a more extensive and structured peer observation study, however, one might wish to look for ways, over a long series of discussions, of ensuring a wide and systematic topic coverage including both teacher and learner behaviour.

### The transcript codings – 'speech act' dimension

The first point to note here is a blurring of the role distinction which might have been expected: for example, not only the observer but also the teacher sometimes evaluates what happened in a lesson, and not only the teacher but also the observer justifies it. This perhaps indicates a high level of mutual supportiveness with the group, with strong desire to convey feelings of solidarity and emphasize the shared features of experience.

Beyond this, we were struck by the wide variation of speech act frequency in the discussions: the differences between the discussions are far more salient than the similarities. For example, Discussions 1B and 4A, with their high frequency of questioning and adverting by the observer, seem to be a very different kind of speech event from 2A and 3A, where these categories are much rarer. (Other untypical figures, such as the high 'back-channelling' rate of the observer in 1B, may reflect individual speech styles.)

What is common to all discussions, however, is a fairly high rate of 'evaluating' acts by the observer (sometimes, as in 2A, only late in the discussion and after frequent invitations to evaluate by the teacher.) Most of these comments were on the observed lesson, although other topics (materials, students, other lessons) were sometimes evaluated. All teachers made one or more evaluative comments on their own lessons, though sometimes not many and always fewer than the observer. Evaluations were in general positive, and any negative comments were tentative and qualified.

The frequency of evaluative comments seems to confirm that peer observation is always likely to be a partially evaluative process, and that, although one can mitigate this by emphasizing non- judgmental aspects, one cannot, and perhaps should not want to, eliminate it entirely.

### General Conclusions

Our first, and unsurprising, conclusion is that the peer observation was worth doing. Teachers did appreciate the opportunity, surprisingly rare in most professional lives, to observe another teacher's lesson and to be observed without any context of evaluation or bureaucratic requirement.

Second, and less certain *a priori*, the coding systems seemed to be of some value. Every professional in the area of systematic observation knows that all existing systems are far from ideal, sometimes difficult to apply – especially to classes taught by modern methods – and not always yielding insights, and the observer comments amply confirmed this. Nonetheless, observers did persevere with systems, often filling in coding sheets very fully – perhaps more fully than we had expected – and showing great resourcefulness in taking the systems as a starting point for more open-ended comments on topics of major interest.

Our third conclusion relates to the low inter-coder reliability on our 'speech-act' dimension. It seems either that we are unusually incompetent in recognising illocutionary force, or, more probably, that what is said in discussions of this type is even more polysemic (multi-functional) than one would generally suppose. This could be a fruitful area for further research.

Fourthly, despite these uncertainties of pragmatic detail, the general goodwill, enthusiasm, mutual supportiveness and professional commitment of the teachers was very much in evidence, as was the structured and principled nature of the curriculum which they were implementing.

Fifthly, it seems that further peer observation, although not an urgent priority, would be of potential benefit to the course, to those of the eight teachers still working on it and to others who have replaced some of them. As usual in such research, any second round of observation could profitably be made slightly more selective and structured, building on the findings of this pilot study. Post-lesson discussion could be similarly guided, with a wide and systematic topic coverage including both teacher and learner behaviour.

## Acknowledgement

We would like to thank the teachers who took part in this project – Wendy Ball, Cathy Benson, Sue Fraser, Marie Gilroy, Liam Rodger, Paul Snookes and Richard Warner.

# References

Bowers, R. (1980) *Verbal Behaviour in the Language Teaching Classroom*. PhD Thesis, University of Reading.

Brown, G. (1975) *Microteaching*. London: Methuen.

Edge, J. (1992) Co-operative development. *ELT Journal* 46,1, 62-70.

Fanselow, J.F. (1977) Beyond Rashomon – conceptualizing and describing the teaching act. *TESOL Quarterly* 11, 17-39.

Fr^hlich, M., Spada, N. and Allen, P. (1985) Differences in the communicative orientation of L2 classrooms'. *TESOL Quarterly* 19, 27-56.

Lockhart, C. (1990) Co-operative teacher development: new observations on observation. *Perspectives* 2, 43-57.

Underhill, A. (1992) The role of groups in developing teacher self-awareness. *ELT Journal* 46, 1, 71-80.

# 9 The European, the Engineer and the Language Teacher: The language education of a bilingual professional

ALISON PIPER
*University of Southampton*

## Introduction

There are three people in my title, so I will start with three quotations:

> The cultivation of positive attitudes to language learning among the students and staff in all disciplines and the encouragement of a wide range of language usage in the academic and social life of the institution' (should be a matter of policy in an establishment of higher education in the European Community).

> The Working Party 'sent a letter to a number of the Engineering Institutions asking about attitudes to language teaching in Engineering courses' after which there was in many cases a lengthy silence. A number explained that 'their Institutions had never discussed the matter before'... and we therefore had to wait until the relevant Committees had met.

> I teach German to Engineering students but I'm all on my own. Who else is doing this?

The first is a statement from the European Commission in their 1991 Memorandum on Higher Education (European Commission 1991:34), the second from a 1990 Working Party of the Engineering Professors' Conference charged with producing a report entitled 'The role of language teaching in Engineering courses' (Tuck 1990), and the third is a comment from a younger member of the British Association for Applied Linguistics made to me after the original of this paper was delivered. Taken together they act as a backdrop to the paper, which is divided into two parts. Firstly, I examine the progress that has been made in higher education in teaching foreign languages to non-specialist linguists, in this case Engineering students, and the movement towards giving the Engineering profession a European dimension. Secondly, I propose four tasks which face Modern and Applied Linguists in carrying

83

Graddol, D and Thomas, S. (1994)
*Language in a Changing Europe,*
Clevedon: BAAL and Multilingual Matters

these developments further, which I suggest provide an agenda for progress.

# The 'Europeanising' of Higher Education

Like the discipline of Modern Languages itself, courses and academic structures oriented towards Europe are long established in British higher education. What is new is the growth in this area, academically in new kinds of language programmes and 'European Studies' and administratively in the appointment of staff to set up European or international 'offices'.

### What is happening in foreign language learning?

One sign of this new orientation, although one that can extend beyond merely European concerns, is the growth of institution-wide language programmes, originally and more colloquially called 'Languages for All'. This movement is now large enough to have set up its own annual conference, the first of which was held at Wolverhampton Polytechnic in 1991. In Thomas's 1992 report for the CNAA, he concludes that out of the 83 HE institutions who responded to his survey, over 29,000 students could be categorised as non-specialist linguists (Thomas 1992). My own impression is that the number of such students who make more than a fleeting introductory commitment to foreign language learning seems to have settled down at an average of about 10 per cent of an institution's student body at any one time. This total is not all accounted for by participants in 'Languages for All' programmes. Nationally there is a wide range of different course types on offer, ranging from the general to the specific purpose and from the voluntary 'bolt-on' programme to the integrated degree option or combined honours scheme.

All this indicates some degree of national commitment to foreign language learning. I shall argue, however, that this commitment has perhaps inevitably focused on concern with new resourcing rather than with establishing a strong theoretical base, and that the hard work of many Modern and Applied Linguists working in this area needs to be coordinated and academically strengthened.

### What is happening in Engineering formation?

Foreign language learning for Engineers has grown up, like most new developments, out of individual enthusiasms which have then been supported at inter-departmental and institutional level. Universities such as Bath, Coventry, Essex, Nottingham and Southampton come to mind, where Scientists and Engineers can integrate continental

European experience and/or specialised language learning into their degree programmes.

As evidenced by my introductory quotation from the Engineering Professors' conference, there is within the profession itself only patchy progress towards a more European approach to what is now often known as 'formation'. There are very many cross-European contacts and partnerships between individuals and institutions, but these exist mostly for purposes of joint research and development. There is also an international title, the *Eur Ing*, which can be obtained by British Chartered Engineers whose competence is attested by the FEANI (Féderation Européene d'Associations Nationales d'Ingénieurs) (see Hector 1991). Documentation in English on the subject of formation, however, is scarce, although this may possibly be a national or linguistic phenomenon since I suspect, but have not been able as yet to track down, a significant literature in German. In several extended searches of databases I have only identified one source of commentary in the form of the *European Journal of Engineering Education*. This is published in the UK under the auspices of SEFI (Société Européene pour la Formation des Ingénieurs) and with no British name on the journal committee although many contributions from British academics. I have also not managed to locate a single University library so far which subscribes to it. This lack of available literature means that whatever activity is going on is difficult to track down.

## Tasks for Language Educators

### Establishing a knowledge base

In his study of 'academic tribes and territories', which includes Engineers, Becher points out that there is an 'almost total neglect of these areas in terms of any documentation of their cultures'. This neglect 'may be connected with the fact that they are far from easy to demarcate from their surrounding domains of professional practice' (Becher 1989:32). Regardless of the reasons, however, Modern Linguists are very different people from Engineers, and we need much more knowledge about the profession, its entrants and practitioners, their various objectives and career patterns, and their cross-national differences and similarities.

Cross-cultural differences add a particular complication to the process of internationalising Engineering formation. One investigation comparing the higher education systems in which various countries of Western Europe educate their Engineers has used Hofstede's 'four dimensions of culture' to identify important dissimilarities between them, particularly in 'power distance' and 'uncertainty avoidance'

(Mainwaring and Markowski 1991). These researchers believe that 'profound differences of training, background and practice exist and that culture-specific notions can lead to deep-seated misunderstandings pervading the many international, cooperative ventures in engineering (ibid:301). This is a view supported by the national stereotyping volunteered by some of Becher's UK Engineering respondents: the French use an absolutist approach, the Americans a comparative approach and German mechanical Engineers are heavy handed (1989:22).

There are at least two significant contrasts between the continental European tradition of Engineering and the British one. The first is to do with education and status, with the continental profession developing historically in elite institutions under the auspices of central government, producing high status professionals going in France and Germany by the respective formal titles of *ingénieur* and *Ingenieur*. The second is the British tradition of *laissez-faire* decentralisation, with responsibilities for both professional standards and education divided up among separate institutions according to sub-disciplines like Civil or Mechanical Engineering. Mainwaring and Markowski also point out the difference between the significance of the titles *engineer, ingénieur* and *Ingenieur* not only in terms of the relative national prestige attached to their holders but also in terms of professional practice and career destinations, suggesting that France wants more of its ingénieurs to stay with technology while Germany is encouraging its Ingenieure to go into management (1991). Indeed titles like the Eur Ing and cross-national groupings notwithstanding, it is by no means clear how much common ground exists internationally beyond the mutual recognition of formal qualifications and experience, nor how far the notion of a European Engineer is an achievable reality or merely an ideal.

Information is equally lacking on the language practices of Engineering, or indeed of working life in general. One investigation which starts to establish the knowledge base is the LINGUA-supported FLAIR project, which links several European countries in an investigation of the language needs of small and medium-sized companies (Hagen 1993). The project is based on an expansion of the notion of 'needs analysis' into the 'European language audit' model, which emphasises the socio-cultural context of language use. This is a start in the task of documenting not just what parts of other foreign languages Europeans need to use but what they need to know and understand in order to communicate and practise their profession effectively. It is a start which could very usefully be followed by Applied Linguists with reference to other international professions such as Engineering.

## Establishing outcomes

Language audits turn our attention to another feature of the non-specialist linguist debate, namely how far the teaching of the target language in higher education should be instrumentally, and particularly vocationally, motivated. An extreme version of the vocational outcomes of language learning is proposed, unsurprisingly, in the Department of Employment's *National Language Standards* produced in first draft form in 1993 by the Languages Lead Body. These reflect the needs of business and commerce, announcing that 'the new system is based on what people can do rather than on what they know' (Languages Lead Body 1993a:1). The emphasis on doing rather than knowing arises from a competence-based approach to training, described in the Language Standards with reference to the Training Agency's definition in terms of 'the ability to perform... activities' in employment (Languages Lead Body 1993b:78).

For Applied Linguists this is a confusing definition of competence. While I would not wish to propose that our own discipline has a monopoly on the definition of common vocabulary items, such an entangling of *competence* and *performance* is just one symptom of the difficulties which linguists and other professions have in establishing common practices and purposes, both in educational and commercial contexts. One difficulty lies in this apparent dichotomy between outcome as knowledge and outcome as action. This is typified by the kind of question from a member of an Engineering Faculty which goes along the lines of 'why do you need to teach them all this stuff about Spain when all they need is to be able to talk a bit of Spanish and do some Engineering?' While this may be a declining stereotype, it is nevertheless true that Modern Linguists and Engineers rarely start off agreeing on either the level of linguistic competence required for professional competence nor on its nature. This is a problem where ignorance is not necessarily confined to one side or the other, and much mutual work is needed to clarify what kind of language education Engineering students really need.

## Establishing teaching and learning programmes

In spite of these disparate perceptions, Engineers and Modern Linguists have managed to set up a number of joint programmes. What has been achieved is a tribute to all parties concerned. However, localised course development, the pressure to maintain standards and training to meet the accreditation and validation requirements of professional bodies, the heterogeneity of Engineering as a discipline, and the need to attract young people into a notoriously heavyweight educational programme have provided powerful distractions from expanding the European aspects of Engineering formation. Add to this the almost total lack of information about the future destinations and experiences of young British Engineers seeking 'European' careers, and curriculum developers have quite an agenda to pursue.

As far as the learners are concerned, today's young adult language students are undoubtedly more instrumentally motivated than their predecessors, concerned with 'transferable personal skills' as much as with traditional educational values (Parker 1992). To quote a recent Council of Europe survey conducted in Britain, many expect to work in an environment where they will need to use their foreign language, and show a marked inclination for language learning which has an obvious practical purpose in their eyes (King 1993). Such priorities may often conflict with what a Modern Languages Department sees as its traditional educational purpose.

Turning to pedagogy, we might take note of two issues. Firstly the generalised 'Science and Engineering topics' approach, which seems currently to be a popular way of dealing with the heterogeneous groups which normally comprise classes of non-specialist linguists. As an approach, however, it does not address the more subtle and complex issues of working in a foreign language, apparently assuming that these students will somehow acquire insights and skills to make a success of professional life in a foreign discourse community based on what is really a 'general' course or set of materials built around 'special purpose' topics. This is not to say that many teachers are not aware of these limitations, but for people often working in isolation and where there is no published language learning material, it may be no more than a practical solution in a pioneering endeavour. In tandem with the topic-based approach is the growing central pressure to technologise education, a process somehow magically supposed to make it cost less and encourage independent learning more. It is interesting that the Council of Europe survey mentioned above reveals a marked disinclination on the part of young adult language students for learning activities which could be characterised as 'self-directed'. This is directly at odds with the whole paraphernalia of open access Language Centres, multi-media resources and notions of self-directed learning which are the paradigms of the moment.

Thus teachers of Modern Languages for specific purposes are people confronting many new demands. They need to acquire knowledge of different fields, to design and teach interdisciplinary courses, to be able to resolve conflicts of interest and principle. And their more traditional skills are now having to be redirected towards developing new pedagogies for themselves and more appropriate learning strategies for their students. As anyone who is in the problematical business of appointing teachers of non-specialist linguist will know, all this brings us to the issue of professional formation. Where are all these experts, and where are they going to come from?

### Establishing a theoretical framework

Professional development for teachers of non-specialist linguists is only possible where there is a satisfactory theoretical framework in which to situate it. As the existing literature makes clear, this has not yet materialised.

As in all disciplines in an early stage of development, most of the documentation is taken up with descriptions of current activity rather than theory building or analysis. To take Engineering first, we find that most of the contents of the already-mentioned European Journal of Engineering Education are descriptions of the design and delivery of course programmes, with the addition of papers on the overall nature of Engineering education in specific countries worldwide. This documentation of 'what is done', both in the classroom and at institutional level, is also a feature of Modern Languages publications which concern work with non-specialist linguists. Two examples are Languages for the world of work (Stevens 1991) and French and the enterprise path (Coleman and Parker 1992), the latter being about higher education and also including more theoretical discussion. At institutional level it is often the questionnaire-based survey which is used to describe 'what is done' in Modern Languages. Such surveys are used both nationally (see Thomas 1992, Rigby and Burgess 1991) and locally, where they may be used to contribute to language audits in which the writers are arguing for institutional resources to extend their teaching base (see, for example, Hanstock 1991 and Piper 1992 for Salford and Southampton Universities respectively). These reports can do no more, though, than identify what can be described and quantified on the basis of easily collectable surface data about current activity.

# An Agenda for Progress

While a few conferences have taken place for institution-wide language programmes and special purposes language teaching, and while important initiatives have started up, the process of discipline development is one on which the practitioners of specialist Modern Languages teaching have scarcely as yet embarked. This is hardly surprising given the newness of their enterprise and their modest resource base. In both this field and that of European Engineering formation, teaching is supported largely by a descriptive literature which focuses on what teachers and training programmes do. It is a literature made up of many individual contributions and overall it pays little attention to underlying assumptions, the development of principles, the needs of the learners and the implications of their future careers, nor to the research which is needed to investigate these matters. While non-specialist language teaching programmes and the new national Language Standards address themselves to generic ideas of 'the Engineer' or 'the needs of industry' as if these were unitary discourse communities, these schemes are designed on the basis of economy and simplicity and do not account for the complexity of the target learner communities.

The descriptive and topic-based approach to modern languages for non-specialist linguists stands in contrast to the field of English for Specific Purposes, where a substantial theoretical basis continues to develop in order to underpin practical applications. Here teachers have built up a discipline with an established research programme in which the complexities of language learning for non-specialist students of English are seriously addressed at both the theoretical and the practical level (e.g. Robinson 1991). Work extends, for example, to the study of disciplinary and professional cultures and, in English for Academic Purposes studies, to genres and their discourse communities. The concept of 'discourse community' as proposed by Swales, with defining characteristics such as 'a broadly agreed set of public goals' and 'a threshold level of members with a suitable degree of relevant content and discoursal expertise' (Swales 1990:27) provides a highly appropriate framework for starting research into the Engineering 'community'.

I would like to hear from readers that this paper paints a picture of exaggerated pessimism, that I have failed either to find the relevant literature or to make contact with the right people, that I have belittled and ignored thriving networks of productive colleagues stretching across the nation. Even though I know that these concerns are shared by many colleagues, if I have got it all wrong then I apologise. If not then I think all those of us who teach Modern Languages for specific purposes should get together, learn from each other and from other disciplines, and start to establish ours as an enterprise which is productive both of good teaching and learning and of good theory and research.

# References

Becher, T. (1989) *Academic tribes and territories*. Milton Keynes: The Society for Research into Higher Education and Open University Press.

Coleman, J.A. and Parker, G. (eds) (1992) *French and the Enterprise Path*. London: Association for French Language Studies in association with the Centre for Applied Language Teaching and Research.

European Comission (1991) *Memorandum on Higher Education in the European Community*. Brussels: Task Force Human Resources, Education, Training, Youth. Commission of the European Communities.

Hagen, S. (ed.) (1993) *Languages in European Business: A regional survey of small and medium-sized companies.* London: City Technology Colleges Trust Limited in association with the Centre for Information on Language Teaching and Research.

Hanstock, J. (1991) *Report of the Foreign Languages Review.* Salford: University of Salford.

Hector, P. (1991) Should British metallurgists become European engineers? *Metals and materials* April 1991, 234.

King, A. (1993) *Languages for Work and Life.* Cambridge: University Language Centre for the Council of Europe.

Languages Lead Body (1993a) *Introduction to the National Language Standards.* London: Languages Lead Body, supported by the Employment Department.

----- (1993b) *National Language Standards.* London: Languages Lead Body, supported by the Employment Department.

Macleod, I.A. (1992) The competence of an Ingenieur. *European Journal of Engineering Education* 17, 361-369.

Mainwaring, D. and Markowski, K. (1991) Cultural factors in the structure and context of European Engineering Studies. *European Journal of Engineering Education* 16, 299-307.

Parker, G. (1992) Enterprise skills. In J.A. Coleman and G. Parker (eds) (1992) *French and the Enterprise Path.* London: Association for French Language Studies in association with the Centre for Applied Language Teaching and Research.

Piper, A. (1992) *Languages in the University of Southampton: A report on the Language Audit carried out by the Director of the Language Centre in 1991.* Southampton: Centre for Language in Education University of Southampton.

Rigby, G. and Burgess R.G. (1991) *Language teaching in Higher Education: A discussion document.* Warwick: Centre for Educational Development Appraisal and Research, University of Warwick.

Robinson, P. (1991) *ESP Today: A practitioner's guide.* New York: Prentice Hall.

Stevens, A. (ed.) (1991) *Languages for the World of Work.* London: Centre for Information on Language Teaching and Research.

Swales, J. (1990) *Genre Analysis.* Cambridge: Cambridge University Press.

Thomas, G. (1992) Survey of European languages in the United Kingdom. *Phase IV of the Review of European Languages and European Studies.* London: Council for National Academic Awards.

Tuck, B. (1990) The role of language teaching in Engineering courses. *Engineering Professors' Conference Occasional Papers,* No.2 Nottingham: University of Nottingham.

# 10 Metalinguistic Knowledge, Language Aptitude and Language Proficiency

DAVID STEEL AND J. CHARLES ALDERSON
*University of Lancaster*

## Introduction

This paper presents a preliminary investigation of the psycholinguistic abilities of first-year undergraduate student learners of French. In particular, it reports on the construction and use of a battery of tests of metalinguistic knowledge, language aptitude, grammatical accuracy in French, and French linguistic proficiency, and explores the relationships amongst these measures with a view to establishing levels of metalinguistic knowledge in incoming undergraduates. The paper reports on pilot work and makes proposals for further research in the light of the results.

According to university modern language teachers, incoming students know little about language and are less accurate in their language use than previous years' students. However, first-year language teaching assumes both knowledge about language and a degree of grammatical accuracy. What is meant by 'knowledge about language' needs to be explored, but it typically includes a knowledge of and ability to use metalanguage appropriately.

Staff impressions of these deficiencies need corroboration, and no empirical evidence was available. The consequences of such deficiencies may be that students need to be taught a metalanguage in secondary school. However, it may be that university teaching should change instead, in order not to rely upon (non-existent) metalinguistic knowledge. A further possibility, however, is that 'knowledge about language' and language proficiency are unrelated.

Communicative language teaching in schools has led to greater ability to use the modern foreign language, but a de-emphasis on accuracy and metalanguage. Knowledge about language is held to be an important component of education in general, and is thought to contribute to language learning. Language aptitude, one key component of which is grammatical sensitivity, is still widely regarded as important in language learning success. The relationship between

92

Graddol, D and Thomas, S. (1994)
*Language in a Changing Europe*,
Clevedon: BAAL and Multilingual Matters

aptitude and knowledge about language is unknown. Bloor's 1986 survey showed low levels of knowledge about language, even for 'linguists', but had no information on the relationship of such lack of knowledge to language proficiency.

In light of the above, several research possibilities present themselves:

1     University foreign language students' supposed lack of metalinguistic knowledge does not exist, and the situation now is in fact no different from previously.

      Alternatively, students' metalinguistic knowledge has indeed declined and is now at a low level.

2     Even if this suspected lack of knowledge can be established it does not bear any relationship to competence in the modern foreign language.

      Alternatively, metalinguistic knowledge does bear such a relationship.

3     If students can be shown to lack the knowledge presupposed, the consequences are that they need to learn it at university, and current assumptions concerning the appropriate methodology for first-year language teaching will need to change.

      Alternatively, they do not need to learn it at university but the methodology of teaching language at university will need to change to avoid the use of metalanguage.

4     In language proficiency, a formal metalinguistic knowledge of grammar is less important than the ability to detect systematic and meaningful patterning in language: language aptitude.

# A pilot study

## Aims

This paper reports on a pilot study designed to begin to explore these and related issues. The aim of the research was to establish levels of:

a)    the metalinguistic knowledge, applied to English and French, of university students of French on entry.

b)    their accuracy in French grammar.

c)    their aptitude for learning language

d)    their proficiency in French, as involved in understanding French texts

e)    their self-assessment of their linguistic abilities in French

and the relationships among these variables.

## Instruments and data collection

A battery of tests was developed, comprising:

a)    a 100-item Test of Metalinguistic Knowledge, for both French and
      English. (Part of this test was based, with permission, on the instrument
      used by Bloor, 1986a, in order to facilitate comparison with his results;
      other sections included metalinguistic items identified by staff of the
      French Department.)

b)    a 45-item Test of Language Aptitude (Part IV of the MLAT, Words in
      Sentences)

c)    a 100-item Test of Grammatical Accuracy in French (consisting of items
      considered important by staff of the French Department, see below).

d)    a questionnaire asking students to self-assess their ability to use French
      in a range of settings

e)    a 50-item standardised Test of French Reading Comprehension
      (constructed by CITO, the Dutch National Testing Agency).

In addition, a bio-data sheet was constructed to collect information
on potentially important background variables such as: age; sex; length
of time spent learning the foreign language; experience of learning
other modern or classical languages; time spent in the country of the
target foreign language; parental example (whether native speaker or
teacher of target language); performance on measures of language
competence at A-Level. This battery was pre-tested on Sixth Year
secondary school pupils studying A Level French. The trialling provided
valuable information on timing and level of difficulty, and in the light of
the trials, the tests were revised. All first- year undergraduates entering
the French section of the Modern Languages Department at Lancaster
University took the test battery in a two-week period in October 1992
(not all students took every section of the battery: see reported n sizes).
In addition, students studying first-year introductory courses in
linguistics took the Bloor part of the Metalinguistic Knowledge test, to
enable comparisons with the Bloor data and with the results of the
French undergraduates.

## Results

The descriptive statistics are as follows:

|                     | Metaling | MLAT | Grammar | French Reading |
|---------------------|----------|------|---------|----------------|
| Number of students  | 128      | 128  | 107     | 102            |
| Number of items     | 100      | 45   | 100     | 50             |
| Mean score          | 59.88    | 22.14| 54.83   | 31.78          |
| Mean as %           | 60%      | 49%  | 55%     | 64%            |
| Standard deviation  | 11.71    | 4.99 | 11.10   | 8.56           |
| Reliability (alpha) | .897     | .687 | .856    | .890           |

*Table 1: Descriptive Statistics*

Reliabilities are entirely satisfactory for this test battery, except for MLAT. This latter finding is somewhat surprising, as the test is standardised and has been widely used for thirty years.

The descriptive statistics reveal that the tests were all of appropriate difficulty for this population and resulted in a reasonable spread of candidates across the range of possible scores. Item analysis revealed a range of item difficulties, as expected, but virtually no items were unsatisfactory because of negative discrimination. It was concluded from the item level data that the tests were satisfactory.

Students were 'weakest' on the Aptitude test, and 'strongest' at reading in French. However, the spread of students on the reading test was quite large: students vary most in their reading abilities. The mean score on the Grammar test of 55% suggests that, if this test reflects what students are supposed to know when they arrive at University, their knowledge is indeed weak. Similarly, if students could have been expected to·'know' the metalanguage in the Metalinguistic Knowledge test, their performance is worrisomely poor.

## Comparisons of performance on the Test of Metalinguistic Knowledge

| Lancaster French (n=128)       | 62.8% |
|--------------------------------|-------|
| Bloor 'Linguists' (n=63)       | 77.5% |
| Lancaster 'non-linguists'      | 50%   |
| Bloor 'non-linguists' (n=175)  | 51.1% |

*Table 2: Comparison of Lancaster 1992 Students with Bloor's 1986 data*

*French students vs students of introductory linguistics at Lancaster*

Levels of metalinguistic knowledge varied considerably in the sample, although all groups do well on a few items (identifying vowels, verbs, nouns, adjectives and subjects). All groups do particularly poorly on some items and rather badly on most items.

The French group is notably better than the other two on 17 out of the 24 questions. The differences Bloor found between linguists and non-linguists were broadly reflected in the differences between French students and students of linguistics. It seems that learners of French have a better metalanguage than other students. (Some might even wish to argue that the study of a foreign language increases one's sensitivity to grammatical categories, and hence performance on this Test of Metalinguistic Knowledge. However, the research was not designed to enable us to investigate this suggestion.)

Nevertheless, it would appear that any instruction that assumed that first year undergraduates knew much more than 'verb', 'noun' and, possibly, 'adjective' would cause students difficulties.

*Comparison with Bloor data*

The differences Bloor found between linguists and non-linguists were replicated at Lancaster, but when Bloor's linguists were compared with the Lancaster French students, the latter were generally weaker. However, when Lancaster non- language students are compared with Bloor's non-linguists, the differences virtually disappear.

Clearly more research is needed, with larger populations from other universities, but it would appear from these comparisons that, assuming comparable ability levels on admission for the two institutions, the metalinguistic knowledge of students of French has declined. However, non-linguists remained at roughly comparable levels of metalinguistic knowledge (which is considerably lower than language students in most linguistic categories). If the populations are equivalent then this might suggest that overall standards have not declined, or that they cannot go much lower. Rather, what has declined is the metalinguistic knowledge of students of French, relative to the rest of the student population.

We again conclude that any instruction that assumed that first year undergraduates understood much more than 'verb', 'noun', 'subject' and, possibly, 'adjective' would cause students difficulties.

### Students' Knowledge of Metalanguage and Grammar

*Metalanguage.*

The Bloor test was only one part of the Metalanguage Test. The latter includes a self-assessment of one's familiarity with grammatical terms, tests of knowledge of English and French grammatical terminology, and the ability to use the terms to identify parts of speech in French texts, as well as Bloor's test of ability to identify parts of speech in English text. An interesting comparison is sub-test 6 – the Bloor items in English – with sub-test 4, which covers similar items but applied to French. The two lists of form classes to be identified in French/ English texts partially overlapped, and the results for overlapping items were:

|                    |      | French | English |
| ------------------ | ---- | ------ | ------- |
| auxiliary verb     |      | 61%    | 54%     |
| adjective          |      | 90%    | 91%     |
| infinitive         |      | 97%    | 73%     |
| preposition        |      | 69%    | 62%     |
| indefinite article |      | 25%    | 34%     |
| past participle    |      | 91%    | 91%     |
| conjunction        |      | 41%    | 56%     |
| finite verb        |      | 49%    | 41%     |
|                    | Mean | 65.4%  | 62.8%   |

*Table 3: Bloor items: French/English*

These results show a tendency for the English items to be easier than the French ones. Although the differences are not marked, the results suggest that being able to apply the grammatical term to English text does not guarantee an ability to apply the same term to a French text.

Sub-test 1 asked students simply to indicate whether they were or were not familiar with certain metalinguistic terms. Of the 30 items, only 10 were reportedly familiar to more than 80% of the students. Particularly unfamiliar were: 'predicate', 'antecedent', 'partitive article' 'relative clause', 'subordinate clause', 'relative pronoun' and 'transitive verb'.

Comparisons are possible between items students claimed to be familiar with and their performance on those items elsewhere in the test. The results are shown in Table 4. In general it appears that students considerably overestimate their familiarity with these grammatical terms. True unfamiliarity is likely to be greater than the results for sub-test 1 suggest.

If teaching is based upon an assumption that students know the terms tested in the Metalinguistic Assessment Test, those assumptions, and possibly that teaching, need to be revised.

|                   | Claimed familiar | Actual correct |
|-------------------|------------------|----------------|
| conjunction       | 72%              | 41/56%         |
| direct object     | 95%              | 46/67%         |
| indefinite article| 59%              | 25/34%         |
| indirect object   | 93%              | 61%            |
| infinitive        | 98%              | 97/73%         |
| noun              | 98%              | 99%            |
| passive voice     | 74%              | 48%            |
| past participle   | 100%             | 91/91%         |
| predicate         | 7%               | 8%             |
| preposition       | 91%              | 69/62%         |
| proper noun       | 69%              | 78%            |
| relative clause   | 35%              | 17%            |
| transitive verb   | 42%              | 12%            |

*Table 4: Claimed familiarity/ actual*

*Grammar Content sub-tests*

The French Grammar test covers a range of different structures and includes a variety of different methods of testing, including a gap-filling test, a translation test, and several transformation tests. Items tested include: gender, plurals, adverbs, special adjectives, superlatives, pronouns, passe compose, relative clauses, verb tenses and possessive adjectives

The most difficult section proved to be sub-test 9: relative clauses, with very weak performance by students. The easiest section by far was sub-test 7: Passé Composé (form). Candidates varied considerably in their abilities on all sections of the test, which discriminated well between weak and strong. If it is thought that students ought to do well on this grammar test, the fact that all means except one are below 70% indicates considerable weakness, but the high variability in performance means that some students do very well, whilst others are very weak, on all sections except the gap-filling.

In short, students vary greatly in the accuracy with which they use French. The interesting question is whether the ability to produce accurate French correlates with a knowledge of metalanguage, or with grammatical sensitivity as measured by the MLAT, or indeed with an ability to understand texts written in French.

## Students' French Comprehension Ability

The results in Table 1 showed the comprehension test to have been the easiest of the battery, but not too easy, with a mean of 64% and a good spread of scores. What is clear from an inspection of item facilities, however, is that this discrimination was a result of speededness: 78% of students failed to get as far as the last two items.

Students did well on the items for the first four texts: most facilities are over 75% (and 5/33 over 90%). In other words, when students did read the texts and respond to the questions, they tended to do so correctly. The problem seems to be that many students read rather slowly. This is interesting in that it suggests that students do understand written French even though some read faster than others. Are the slower readers those who have most problems with grammar or metalanguage, or who have less 'aptitude'?

## Relationship among tests and constructs

In order to explore the relationship among the tests, correlations were calculated. For the 92 students who took all the components of the battery, the results are as follows:

|           | MLAT | Grammar   | French Reading |
|-----------|------|-----------|----------------|
| Metaling  | .435 | .429      | .072 (NS)      |
| MLAT      |      | .203 (NS) | .186 (NS)      |
| Grammar   |      |           | .399           |

*Table 5: Intercorrelations among tests*

These results seem to show that the test of French Reading shows no relationship to knowledge of metalanguage, or to language aptitude as defined by MLAT. The Metalanguage and Aptitude tests, however, do show a moderate inter- relationship, albeit less than might have been expected. The Grammar test relates moderately to the Metalanguage test, but also to the test of French Reading. To explore the relationships further, a factor analysis was conducted, with Varimax rotation.

|                  | Factor 1 | Factor 2 | Commonality |
|------------------|----------|----------|-------------|
| Grammar          | .394     | .721     | .675        |
| French Reading   | -.039    | .906     | .823        |
| Metalang         | .869     | .120     | .770        |
| Aptitude (MLAT)  | .782     | .096     | .620        |
| Eigenvalue       | 1.88     | 1.01     |             |
| Variance %       | 47%      | 25%      |             |

*Table 6 Varimax rotated factor analysis: Two factors, Eigenvalue > 1.0*

This analysis shows that there are two factors underlying these four tests: a metalinguistic factor on which Metalanguage and Aptitude tests load high, and a test of French Reading. The Grammar test is split across the two factors, but with a higher loading on Factor 2 (French Use?) than on the metalinguistic factor.

What the analyses appear to reveal is that the Metalanguage test measures something different from what is measured by the Grammar and Comprehension tests. As was shown by the simple correlation matrix, metalinguistic knowledge and aptitude are related, although not closely. However, there is no relationship between linguistic proficiency defined by the tests we used, and metalinguistic knowledge. Subsequent sections will explore this further by comparing metalinguistic knowledge with self-assessed proficiency and with proficiency as measured by A-Level grades.

### The relationship between self-assessment and test performance

There is little interpretable relationship between the difficulties that students predict for their use of French in a number of different communicative situations, and their ability as measured by the four tests. Students who predict few difficulties do not do better on the tests, nor vice versa.

However, students' assessments of their global ability to use French in the four skills did associate significantly with their test scores.

| self assessed skill/ test | metalanguage | aptitude | grammar | comprehension |
|---|---|---|---|---|
| reading | Yes | No | Yes | Yes |
| writing | Yes | No | No | No |
| listening | Yes | No | No | Yes |
| speaking | No | No | Yes | No |

*Table 7: Association of self-assessed skill with test score (p<.05)*

Table 7 summarises these results, showing that the Aptitude test shows no relationship with self assessment. Interestingly, the Metalanguage test shows the most consistent associations with perceived ability in the skills: with the exception of speaking, those who rate themselves high on a skill tend to score high on the Metalanguage test, and conversely those who rate themselves low tend to score low on the test.

### The relationship among biodata variables and test scores

Crosstabulations were run between biodata and test scores, and some interesting relationships were found. See Table 8.

|                        | Metaling | Aptitude | Grammar | Reading |
|------------------------|----------|----------|---------|---------|
| Language Major         | No       | No       | No      | Yes     |
| Grade A level French   | No       | No       | Yes     | Yes     |
| Sex                    | Almost   | No       | No      | No      |
| # weeks in France      | No       | No       | Yes     | No      |
| Type of sec school     | No       | No       | No      | No      |
| Other A Level Language | No       | No       | No      | No      |
| Grade in above         | No       | No       | No      | No      |
| A Level EngLit         | No       | No       | No      | No      |
| A Level EngLang        | No       | No       | No      | No      |

*Table 8 Associations between bio-data and test scores*

When 'Intended Major' was recategorised as 'Language-related subjects' and 'non-language subjects', there was no relationship between this variable and scores on the Metalanguage, Aptitude or Grammar tests, but there was with the Reading test: students intending to study languages understand French texts somewhat better, but do not do better on Grammar tests, nor have they better aptitude or higher metalanguage scores!

Significant associations were found between A Level French grade and scores on Grammar and Reading tests on the one hand, but not with the Metalanguage or Aptitude tests on the other: students who do better at A Level do not necessarily have better grammatical sensitivity or knowledge of metalanguage, but their accuracy in French grammar and their French reading comprehension are better.

Interestingly, sex was almost significantly associated with Metalanguage scores (p=.051), but not with Grammar, Aptitude or Reading. Number of weeks spent in France was not associated with Metalanguage, Aptitude or even Reading test scores, but it was associated with Grammar test scores. No significant associations were found between type of school attended, and any of the test variables: the school students attend does not make a difference to the test scores.

Whether or not students took another language at A Level has no significant association with any of the test scores, nor does the grade achieved in that other foreign language: doing another language does not increase one's metalinguistic 'ability', aptitude, accuracy in French grammar or comprehension of French. Nor is it the case that doing well at A Level English Literature or English Language will be associated with better scores on any of the tests. Whatever A Level English (Language or Literature) measures, it does not relate to grammatical sensitivity or knowledge of metalinguistic terminology.

### Summary and preliminary conclusions

The correlations between the different components showed only moderate relationships: between metalinguistic knowledge and French grammatical accuracy (.43) and metalinguistic knowledge and language aptitude (grammatical sensitivity) (.44). Proficiency in reading French showed no correlation with either aptitude or metalinguistic knowledge, and only a moderate correlation with French grammatical accuracy (.40). A factor analysis revealed two separate factors: metalinguistic/ aptitude and French proficiency.

Metalinguistic knowledge showed significant associations with self-assessed global proficiency in three of the four skills, but not with other self-assessed components of ability.

Metalinguistic knowledge failed to correlate with scores on the French A-Level exam (arguably the most comprehensive measure of language proficiency we have).

Tentative conclusions are that students can be proficient in the use of French without having aptitude defined as grammatical sensitivity, and without high levels of metalinguistic knowledge. Accuracy in French contributes only moderately to this ability to use French, at least for the purpose of understanding written texts. Although metalinguistic knowledge showed some relationship to accuracy in French, its contribution to proficiency defined by a reading test, by A-Level results and by self-assessment seems to be minimal.

# Limitations and further research

The results of the pilot study revealed a need to refine the test instruments. For tests of French accuracy, one possibility might be to include methods like editing tests, multiple choice tests, even tests of writing or translation.

The range of tests of linguistic proficiency should be widened from tests of reading to include tests of listening and writing ability.

The Test of Metalinguistic Knowledge needs revision to remove inefficient items, and to improve content coverage. In addition, one might argue that the restricted definition of metalinguistic knowledge should be widened.

The Grammatical Sensitivity component of aptitude should be complemented with measures of Inductive Language Learning Ability.

The representativeness of the Lancaster pilot study results for undergraduate students of French more generally is obviously questionable. A further study would need to cover other institutions.

The proposed follow-up study would allow:

1    Systematic comparison of levels of metalinguistic knowledge from Bloor (1986a and c), and the results of this pilot study.

2    Widening of the database on metalinguistic knowledge to cover the intakes of first-year undergraduate students of French in a range of institutions.

3    Comparison of a range of measures of linguistic ability with A-Level results in French and other language subjects.

4    Relation, for a larger, fairly homogeneous sample, of levels of metalinguistic knowledge to levels of accuracy in French, French proficiency and language aptitude.

5    Consideration of the pedagogic and curricular implications of the resultant findings about levels of knowledge, accuracy and proficiency.

# References

Bloor, T. (1986a) What do language students know about grammar? *British Journal of Language Teaching*, Vol 24 Winter 1986:157-60

Bloor, T. (1986b) Variation and Prescriptivism in English: Modern language students' attitudes to some sociolinguistic issues. *CLIE Working Papers* Number 7

Bloor, T. (1986c) University Students' Knowledge about Language. *CLIE Working Papers* Number 8.

# 11 Communicative Conflict in the 'New' Germany: Adaptation and change in public discourse

PATRICK STEVENSON
*University of Southampton*

## Introduction

For many observers, the sudden demise of the GDR inevitably entailed the end of research on East – West linguistic contrasts. It was, of course, true that many forms of public discourse ceased quite abruptly when the political institutions that they inhabited were closed down, and these were then 'only' of historical interest. It was also true though that in the so-called *Umbruchsphase* or transition period itself public language became the focus of renewed attention: on the one hand, there were the 'new' public discourses of the ruling Socialist Unity Party's *Selbstrettungsversuche* (desperate attempts at survival: see Good, 1991) and of the newly legitimised opposition (such as *Neues Forum*), and on the other hand there were the various articulations of popular protest (such as the slogans chanted by the crowds or displayed on banners during the mass demonstrations in Leipzig, Berlin and other major cities). However, these were all temporary phenomena, and they have been extensively chronicled and analysed (see, for example, Fix, 1990; Hellmann, 1990; Kinne, 1991; Lang, 1990; Reiher, 1992; Volmert, 1992).

But this is not the whole story. Other forms of public language that constitute(d) the substance of everyday social life have been widely ignored: I am thinking, for example, of routine spoken interaction as a form of social behaviour in public and semi-public contexts, and of written texts produced for either general or particular public consumption other than through the medium of state-controlled newspapers or official documents. Of course, these were precisely the forms of language that were least accessible to systematic study, but they are equally clearly the channels through which real social relationships were enacted.

Graddol, D and Thomas, S. (1994)
*Language in a Changing Europe,*
Clevedon: BAAL and Multilingual Matters

It has become commonplace to observe not only a sense of disillusion and disorientation amongst the population of what used to be the GDR, but also the obstinate refusal of both communities to 'obey' the simple logic of former Chancellor Willy Brandt's fatally unprophetic pronouncement in November 1989, that 'what belongs together is now growing together' (*jetzt wächst zusammen, was zusammen gehört*). There are many reasons for this, but I would like to consider here the justification for seeing the continuing East/West dichotomy in part as a problem of intercultural communication, the central question being: why is the supposed 'common bond' of language creating an invisible wall between the two communities?

Clearly, as Schlosser (1991) says, it is too late to reconstruct the everyday speech patterns of GDR times. However, we do now have unlimited access to speakers in what still appear to be two only partially overlapping speech communities, and we can also begin to gather written material of a semi-public nature that can show more comprehensively 'where East Germans are coming from' in terms of the communicative and discursive conditions of everyday life, and which can be studied against what has replaced it in order to reveal the extent to which East Germans have had to enter a (for them) wholly new 'discourse world'. There are many questions that could now be pursued in this context, but the overriding condition of post-unification Germany is that accommodation to the 'other' on all levels, including the linguistic/communicative, is to be a one-way process. Two possible lines of enquiry that suggest themselves are therefore:

i)    how do East Germans come to terms with burdens imposed on them by the myriad forms of written discourse that confront them on a daily basis, such as social security forms, insurance documents, rental agreements on the one hand, and media products such as newspapers and commercial advertising on the other?

ii)   how do East Germans react to the new communicative conditions and demands in specific contexts of spoken interaction, on the public (e.g. parliamentary debates, television interviews), semi-public (e.g. classroom or workplace), and private levels?

In the following sections, I shall consider some specific issues within these two general sets of problems, drawing on recent initial research in the Brandenburg town of Cottbus.

# Written Texts in Institutional Contexts: Education and the school

The school played a central role in the construction of the socialist society of the GDR, as it was the institution charged with the formation of 'allseitig entwickelte sozialistische Schülerpersönlichkeiten' (all-round socialist pupils). This was a process that went far beyond the mere 'education' of children: school was both a Lerngemeinschaft (learning community) and a Lebensgemeinschaft (community for living) (Schmidt 1991), a social project on a grand scale in which pupils, teachers and parents were (at least theoretically) constantly involved.

This is not the place to discuss the extent to which this ambitious community project was actually implemented: the important point here is the detailed articulation of functions and relationships that made Party and state, school, youth organisations and families explicitly and necessarily bound up together within the process (see also Helwig 1991). Some measure of the 'discursive penetration' of the ideological programme within the institution can be gained from the mass of documents that were generated routinely in the course of everyday life in schools, just two examples of which are discussed below. These texts, taken from a vast collection in the archives of a school in Cottbus, illustrate how in various forms the official discourse percolated down from one level to another to permeate the entire discursive field.

### Text 1

**Arbeitsplan des Fachzirkels Deutsch – Schuljahr 1983/84**
I. ZIELSTELLUNG Mit der Einführung neuer Lehrpläne im Fach Deutsche Sprache und Literatur erhöhen sich die Anforderungen, die an jede Unterrichtsstunde gestellt werden. Es gilt, die Qualität des Literaturunterrichts zu verbessern und – wie Margot Honecker auf der zentralen Direktorenkonferenz formulierte – 'die dem literarischen Kunstwerk innewohnenden Möglichkeiten für die Persönlichkeitsentwicklung' zu nutzen. Der Literaturunterricht soll stärker als bisher einen wirkungsvollen Beitrag zur kommunistischen Erziehung der Schüler leisten. Daher sind im Rahmen der Arbeit des Fachzirkels Deutsch alle Möglichkeiten auszuschöpfen, die einen erziehungswirksamen und bildungseffektiven Unterricht fördern. [...] Dabei stehen sich alle Kollegen mit Rat und Tat zur Seite.

**[Plan of work for the German Section – School Year 1983/84**
I. OBJECTIVES With the introduction of the new syllabuses for German Language and Literature, increased demands will be made of each lesson. It will be necessary to improve the quality of literature teaching and – as Margot Honecker put it at the central conference of head teachers – to make use of 'the opportunities for personality development that are inherent in literary works of art'. Literature teaching is to make a more effective contribution than in the past to the communist education of the pupils. Therefore, in the context of the work of the German Section full use is to be made of all possible ways of promoting educationally effective teaching. [...] All colleagues will give each other their full support in achieving this.]

This text is taken from a paper written by the head of the German section, outlining the aims and objectives of the coming year's work. Its immediate target audience is therefore the small group of teachers working in this section, but any text committed to paper and circulated even within such a small group would automatically become part of the public domain. This double status of texts like this has interesting consequences for their writers, and the extract reproduced here shows very clearly how practical pedagogical business was conducted within the frame of the official discourse.

The thrust of the section head's message to her colleagues is that they must consider how to implement the new syllabuses that have just been introduced. However, this simple point has to be filtered through a number of central ideological tenets in order to conform to the norm for public texts on educational policy. The first of these is that all aspects of the process of social construction make ever increasing demands on those involved, and so the text begins with the conventional assertion that the introduction of new syllabuses will (by implication: inevitably) raise the demands made of every class. Similarly, just as the quality of washing machines or any other consumer product was always 'good but not yet good enough', so the text insists (with a superfluous but routine reference to the then Education Minister Margot Honecker) that the quality of literature teaching must be improved, and specifically that it should make a more 'effective contribution to the communist education of the pupils'. However, the logical connector daher (therefore) then provides a spurious link between this obligatory 'mission statement' and the more general (and quite possibly contradictory) assertion that 'everything should be done to promote effective teaching'. The final sentence then returns to the official mode with the standard insistence on mutual support within the teaching collective.

### Text 2

**Rechenschaftsbericht der Klasse 10b**
Im vergangenen Schuljahr erfüllten wir unseren Arbeitsplan nur teilweise. Wir veranstalteten zwar einen Kuchenbasar, dessen Erlös wir für die Solidarität spendeten, und eine Weihnachtsfeier, welche wohl bei allen Begeisterung fand, aber es kamen z.B. ein gemeinsamer Kinobesuch sowie eine Radtour zu kurz, auch mit einer Einladung eines Arbeiterveterans klappte es nicht ganz. [...] Man darf natürlich auch die politischen Gespräche, welche unser Agitator Peter Schneider leitete, nicht vergessen. Den Lehrgang für Zivilverteidigung schlossen wir mit guten Ergebnissen ab. Einige Schüler erhielten wegen ihrer Einsatzbereitschaft eine Auszeichnung. [...] In der 10. Klasse muß noch mehr darauf geachtet werden, daß es nicht dazu kommt, daß ständig dieselben FDJ-ler an freiwilligen Einsätzen teilnehmen. Der Arbeitsplan der 10. Klasse müßte also noch konkreter die Arbeit der einzelnen Schüler kennzeichnen.

**Annual Report of Class 10b**
In the past school year we only partially fulfilled our plan of work. We did organise a cake sale, the proceeds from which we donated to the solidarity fund, and a Christmas party, which was enthusiastically received by all, but e.g. a group visit to the cinema and a bicycle trip didn't really come off, and the invitation of a veteran of work didn't quite work out. [...] The political discussions, which our political instructor Peter Schneider led, should of course not be forgotten. We successfully completed the course in civil defence. A number of pupils received a commendation for their willingness to serve. [...] In the 10th class attention must be paid to ensuring that it is not always the same FDJ (Free German Youth) members who take part in voluntary activities. The work plan of the 10th class should therefore specify more concretely the work of individual pupils.]

It was the job of each class to produce an annual report on its activities, written by the pupils themselves but obviously under the guidance and supervision of the class teacher (see also Straßner 1985). These texts are therefore also a form of public language and thereby subject to the same kinds of constraint as the texts produced by members of staff. Like Text 1, but in a different way, this text operates on two different levels. It is ostensibly an account of the class's activities and achievements and its attempts to fulfil its 'work plan'. In keeping with the nature of these tasks and objectives, it is composed within the frame of the standard discourse: 'we only partially fulfilled our work plan', 'a number of pupils received a commendation for their willingness to serve', 'the work plan of the 10th class should therefore specify more concretely the work of individual pupils'. It also focuses on key prescribed activities such as collecting money for 'solidarity funds' (i.e. to support the struggle of socialists in other countries), looking after 'veterans of work' (i.e. retired workers who had received commendations for their contribution to the development of the socialist society), and attending 'discussions' with their *Agitator* (political activist, instructor). However, the seriousness that the writer seeks to achieve is undermined by the occasional lapse into a colloquial style ('the invitation of a veteran of work didn't quite work out') and by the juxtaposition of earnest and mundane activities ('we did organise a cake sale, the proceeds of which we donated to the solidarity fund, ...').

The features I have drawn attention to features in these examples are familiar ones in the kinds of public texts that were widely accessible and extensively studied in GDR times. My object here was to show, taking a single domain, how texts of all kinds and of varying degrees of public orientation were formulated within a highly specified set of discursive conventions. Future research could begin with an analysis of how writing practices have changed following the introduction of new school forms, curricula and internal organisation and in the context of renegotiated relationships between pupils, teachers and parents.

# The Destabilisation of Speech Behaviour: Adaptation and accommodation

It was often asserted in the past that East and West Germans could be identified by their speech behaviour (i.e. not merely by the use of specific vocabulary or regional accents, but by what Jens Reich, one of the leading oppositional figures in the late GDR, calls Denkschablonen, patterns (literally 'templates') of thought: see Reich 1991). While attempts to investigate this empirically (e.g. Schlobinski, 1987: 201-2, but see also Liebe Reséndiz, 1992 and my discussion below) have generally proved inconclusive, the belief persists and constitutes one of the main devices for identifying the 'other' Germans.

Random observation suggests that on the strictly linguistic level by no means all distinctive GDR forms have been withdrawn from circulation, despite the now already widespread currency of Western norms. It is impossible to tell whether individual instances are attributable to a lack of awareness on the part of the speakers or to consciously divergent behaviour. What does seem to be clear is that the higher 'market value' associated with speech patterns imported from West Germany has destabilised speech behaviour in the East to the extent that whether or not to adopt these new patterns has become an issue in the process of coming to terms with the new reality. Market forces militate against generally divergent behaviour, but linguistic accommodation takes various different forms and the degree to which it is successful also varies considerably.

The significance of persisting contrasts in patterns of speech behaviour lies in the ways in which they are nominated as key markers, no longer of national, but rather of social difference. Therefore, individual and collective *perceptions* and the responses they generate in terms of influencing behaviour are at least as important as objectively identifiable characteristics. A recent pilot study of perceptions and attitudes amongst teenagers and their parents in Cottbus revealed an extraordinary uniformity of responses, both in terms of attempts at descriptive contrasts and in evaluative terms. West Germans were considered to have a slower, more emphatic speech style and a wider vocabulary, to be more skilled at speaking and more self-confident. Their speech was characterised on the one hand as more refined, more elegant, and more sophisticated, but on the other hand as long-winded and pretentious, with a predilection for foreign (especially of course English) words and elaborate, self-indulgent display ('unheimliches Theater', as one informant put it). There is a pervasive sense of insecurity in the ambivalence of their attitudes, that is very similar to the attitudes towards Berlin speech found by Dittmar et al (1986) in the early 1980s.

They are frequently scathing about the supercilious speech behaviour
of (particularly young) West Germans:

> ... Sprücheklopfer, die in Westdeutschland in der Szene sind und hier in
> Ostdeutschland genau so cool wirken wollen wie die da drüben. [... big-
> mouths who are part of the scene in West Germany and want to appear
> just as cool in East Germany as them 'over there.]

but while sometimes conceding a sense of inferiority, they are typically
defensive about their own identity:

> Ich schäme mich nicht, daß ich aus dem Osten komme, aber wenn ich
> drüben bin, will ich nicht auffallen. [I'm not ashamed of coming from the
> East, but when I'm 'over there' I don't want to stand out.]

Above all, there is a strong sense that West Germans know how to
project a powerful personal image:

> Die Westdeutschen sprechen viel mehr, sie wissen genau, wie sie sich
> geben sollen, gestisch und mimisch, und das schüchtert dann die
> Ostdeutschen ein bißchen ein. [The West Germans talk a lot more, they
> know exactly how to present themselves, using gestures and facial
> expressions, and that is a bit intimidating for East Germans.]

and more generally that for West Germans spoken interaction is more
about establishing personal credentials in terms of 'experiences
consumed' than about establishing personal relationships in terms of
'feelings experienced':

> Die Westler erzählen mehr, was sie gehört haben und was sie erfahren
> haben, während die Ostler mehr so Gefühle äußern. [The West Germans
> tend to talk about what they've heard and what they've done, while the
> East Germans tend to express their feelings.]

## Conclusion

As I hope to have shown, the closing of one chapter in the study of
German-German difference does not mean that the whole story has
been told. Just as unification created at least as many social problems as
it solved, so the removal of formal barriers between the two speech
communities has only revealed the extent and depth of the
communicative differences that continue to divide them. I have tried to
argue that the sharp historical switch in terms of political formations
was not accompanied by a similarly abrupt change in cultural practices,
and that the often discordant voices of German-German interaction
can at least in part be accounted for as a clash between problems of
intercultural communication and a resistance to what many still
perceive as cultural colonialism. Within the constraints of this paper I
could only offer some preliminary considerations of these issues, but I
hope this may provide a basis for a future research agenda.

## Acknowledgement

(I would like to acknowledge the financial assistance provided by the British Academy, which enabled me to undertake much of the research on which this paper is based. I would also like to thank the many people in the former GDR, especially Elfi Ransch and her colleagues, who gave so much of their time discussing the issues raised here; and I am grateful to Alison Piper for comments on an earlier draft of this paper.)

# References

Dittmar, N., Schlobinski, P. and Wachs, I. (1986) *Berlinisch. Studien zum Lexikon, zur Spracheinstellung und zum Stilrepertoire.* Berlin: Berlin Verlag Arno Spitz.

Fix, U. (1990) Der Wandel der Muster – der Wandel im Umgang mit Mustern. *Deutsche Sprache* 4/90, 332-47.

Good, C. (1991) *Language and Totalitarianism: The case of 'East Germany.* Inaugural lecture, University of Surrey (UK), 27 November 1991.

Hellmann, M.W. (1990) DDR-Sprachgebrauch nach der Wende: eine erste Bestandsaufnahme. *Muttersprache* 2-3/90, 266-286.

Helwig, G. (1991) Erziehung in der DDR zwischen öffentlichem Anspruch und Familie. In H.D. Schlosser (ed) *Kommunikationsbedingungen und Alltagssprache in der ehemaligen DDR.* Hamburg: Buske.

Kinne, M. (1991) DDR-Deutsch und Wende-Sprache. *Der Sprachdienst* 2/91, 49-54.

Lang, E. (1990) *Wendehals und Stasi-Laus. Demosprüche aus der DDR.* Munich: Heyne.

Liebe Resendiz, J. (1992) Woran erkennen sich Ost- und Westdeutsche? In K. Welke, W.W. Sauer and H. Glück (eds) *Die deutsche Sprache nach der Wende.* Hildesheim: Olms.

Reich, J. (1991) Ost ist Ost und West ist West. über die kulturellen und seelischen Konflikte in Deutschland. *Frankfurter Rundschau* 23 March 1991, p.7.

Reiher, R. (1992) 'Wir sind das Volk'. Sprachwissenschaftliche überlegungen zu den Losungen des Herbstes 1989. In A. Burkhardt and K.P. Fritzsche (eds) *Sprache im Umbruch.* Berlin, NY: de Gruyter.

Schlobinski, P. (1987) *Stadtsprache Berlin. Eine soziolinguistische Untersuchung.* Berlin, NY: de Gruyter.

Schlosser, H.D. (1991) Notwendige Rückblicke auf eine historisch gewordene Kommunikationsgemeinschaft. In H.D. Schlosser (ed) *Kommunikationsbedingungen und Alltagssprache in der ehemaligen DDR.* Hamburg: Buske.

Schmidt, G. (1991) Lehrersein in der DDR – Das Lehrerbild in der Deutschen Lehrerzeitung. In H.D. Schlosser (ed). *Kommunikationsbedingungen und Alltagssprache in der ehemaligen DDR.* Hamburg: Buske.

Straßner, E. (1985). 'Ich trage die neue Welt in mir'. Argumentationsstrategien angeleitet schreibender Kinder in der DDR. In F. Debus, M.W. Hellmann and H.D. Schlosser (eds) *Sprachliche Normen und Normierungsfolgen in der DDR.* Hildesheim: Olms.

Volmert, J. (1992) Auf der Suche nach einer neuen Rhetorik. In A. Burkhardt and K.P. Fritzsche (eds) *Sprache im Umbruch.* Berlin, NY: de Gruyter.

# 12 Peer and Parental Pressure within the Sociolinguistic Environment: An Anglo-French comparative study of teenage foreign language learners

ANDREA S. YOUNG
*Aston University*

## Introduction

The predominantly monolingual nature of the British population is being increasingly remarked upon and criticised. Within the context of a multilingual, multicultural Europe, why do we stubbornly hang onto our shameful reputation as the linguistic dunces of the community? The significance of our reluctance to learn foreign languages needs to be explored in terms of motivational intensity and attitudes towards foreign language learning (FLL) and the influences affecting these. In France, even young school children within the state school system demonstrate a maturity of outlook and an understanding of the issues related to foreign language learning:

> ...well, there's going to be the opening up of borders and as well as that it's a language that we have to know now because... it's used everywhere...so everyone's thinking about that. (14 year old French girl: Young, 1991: appendix B, page 103)

This positive attitude towards foreign language learning appears to be mirrored in French society at large; the media nurturing such attitudes and often linking this theme to pro-European policies.

In England, both the lack of such stimulation and support and the simultaneous proliferation of comments such as: everyone speaks English, we don't need to learn foreign languages is astounding. Part of the responsibility for such negative attitudes lies with the tabloid press: 'Europe needs plain English' (Daily Mail headline 4/11/91). In this article readers are told that '...English must become the sole official

112

Graddol, D and Thomas , S. (1994)
*Language in a Changing Europe,*
Clevedon: BAAL and Multilingual Matters

language for the Community'. Such linguistic imperialism does nothing to promote FLL and can give rise to very negative preconceptions and stereotypes (Byram, 1991).

Conflicting attitudes observed in the general public and media in both societies would suggest that perceived foreign language needs in Great Britain differ dramatically from those in France. French in Britain is often relegated to at best a specialist's subject, only necessary for certain specific professions, or at worst a holiday language. This attitude is reflected in such comments as:

> ...I don't like it ... it's all right for the people that are going to take up a career like couriering or something like that and be a courier or an airline pilot, but not for the people who don't really want it ... it's a waste of a lesson. (14 year old English boy: Young, 1991:121)

This led me to pose the question: Why do English school children lack motivation for FLL compared to French children? Subsequent key questions need to be raised, with the aim of uncovering explanations as to why and how such differing stances towards FLL come into existence:

1    What is the origin of FLL motivation for pupils attending French and English schools?

2    What is the nature of attitudes towards foreign language learning held by both French and English pupils?

3    What differences exist between French and English pupils in relation to FLL?

4    What are the influences involved in attitude formation and the development of motivation in FLL?

The present paper is concerned with the final question.

# Motivation, attitudes and the sociolinguistic environment

Most work on motivation towards FLL depends on research carried out by Gardner and Lambert (Gardner and Lambert, 1959; 1972) which deals primarily with the linking of attitudes, motivation and achievement. Two different sorts of motivation were identified and defined; *integrative* deriving from a wish to integrate with the target language's culture and society and *instrumental* concerned with acquiring the target language as an instrument, a means to an end, such as to improve career prospects. Gardner and Lambert's initial studies indicated that integratively motivated students were likely to be more successful than instrumentally motivated students. However, these results, pertaining to adults in a Canadian bilingual context, were later contradicted by their 1972 study of adult learners of English in the differently bilingual Philippines. Lukmani's study of Marathi speaking high school students of English in India (Lukmani, 1972) also found that instrumental motivation correlated best with success.

Many other surveys have been conducted and papers published in this field (Burstall, 1970; 1978; Porcher, 1983; Dörnyei, 1990; Gardner and MacIntyre, 1991) and the relative importance of integrative/instrumental motivation has been discussed extensively by all parties with varying conclusions. Universal concepts which do not take into account the role of context may be too simplistic (Gardner, 1985). Different situations produce, not surprisingly, different motivations for FLL. Comparison and contrast between two contexts might clarify the application of the instrumental/integrative dichotomy; as might therefore the relevance of the dichotomy to children of compulsory school age.

A major feature of Gardner's socio-educational model of FLL is his distinction between attitudes and motivation. In fact, Gardner distinguishes three components in motivation: *desire, attitudes,* and *drive.*

Attitudes therefore, form part of that complicated individual patchwork of variables which influence performance in foreign language learning. Language cannot be considered as some sort of neutral linguistic code, as it is intimately linked with its speakers' sense of identity and community, its culture (in both the sociological and aesthetic sense) and the nature of its use. Consequently, attitudes towards the language itself, its speakers and culture become systematically involved in FLL. Such attitudes can be influenced by the learner's social context, that is to say his/her family, friends and the society in which he/she lives.

There is a wealth of possible influences which may affect the individual in the formation of attitudes towards FLL. Variables such as personality, differences in cognitive style, level of intelligence and language aptitude play important roles in the individual's orientation (Gardner and MacIntyre, 1991), attitudes and motivation towards FLL. As much of the adolescent's day is spent at school, intrinsic variables (Harmer, 1983) including factors such as physical conditions, teaching methods, teacher-pupil rapport and successful and enjoyable learning experiences will be a major source of influence upon the learner's attitude towards FLL. Indeed the whole ethos of the particular school in which the individual is educated will be of the utmost importance in the formation of attitudes and aspirations. The perceived role of education, the attitudes of the staff, the status of the foreign language within the school, all contribute in the attitudinal motivational stakes. Such variables, however, although they must not be ignored, are not the primary concern of this paper.

Age is another major factor and as we are examining the 14-15 year old age group, I would suggest that it is the family and friends within the child's immediate environment who play the major role in the development of attitudes. The process of socialisation, which enables adolescents fully to play their part in mature society, is achieved through the transmission of attitudes and values via people, such as parents, peers and members of the community in which the adolescents live. Peer group and parental pressure can motivate through their influence on the development of attitudes. O'Connell (1973) notes the difficulty of separating motivation from such social factors as parental attitudes and aspirations, considering status and social approval to be key factors.

Home environment factors such as socio-economic status and level of education of family members, whether the family offers security, love and support; and to what degree the communication of values, attitudes, opinions and ambitions is achieved will have a direct effect on the child's attitude to FLL. Porcher stresses that: '... it is highly desirable to try to find out what the family's attitude is to foreign languages, and, specifically, to the language under consideration' (Porcher, 1983: 148). He goes on to state that: 'it is clear that if the family and social environment put a high value on learning it has a much better chance of being successful and of appealing to a motivated learner' (Porcher, 1983:149).

During adolescence, self esteem and the need for esteem within the peer group often take on great importance. Harmer notes the shift from parental to peer group pressure as children become adolescents (Harmer, 1983).

Foreign language requirements demanded by employers and whether the child perceives foreign language skills as a prerequisite for future employment will motivate the child to learn. Government policies in the areas of education and foreign policy will also affect foreign language status, as perceived by the child, his/her parents and peers. Inclusion of a foreign language in the national curriculum augments foreign language status. However, this pales somewhat when compared to France, where two foreign languages are the mandatory norm and foreign language learning is allotted 6-8 hours of the weekly curriculum (Minstère de l'Education Nationale, 1985), compared with the recommended 4 periods (approximately 2-3 hours) per week in England (DES, 1990). With respect to foreign policy, pro-European policies and ideas may have the knock-on effect of promoting positive attitudes towards European foreign languages and societies.

## Research Design

The evidence presented in this paper forms part of a larger doctoral research project concerned with motivation and attitudes towards foreign language learning in France and England. My interest lies in the effect of society upon the individual and consequently, the study is made from a sociolinguistic rather than a psycholinguistic perspective. The substance of the research is therefore concerned with motivational and attitudinal factors, especially those rooted in the socio-cultural context, and the differences in these factors between pupils living in Mulhouse, France and her twin town of Walsall in England.

Comparing the two areas we notice that they share a number of key characteristics: the two towns have similarly sized populations, the Mulhouse agglomeration numbering 226,298 inhabitants (1992 Town Hall figures), the Walsall population 259,488 (1991 Census); both towns grew up around the local manufacturing industries, thus sharing a long and rich industrial tradition and finally, their economic positions, 8.9% unemployment in Walsall (1991 Census), 12.2% in Mulhouse (1990 Census). Successive waves of immigration experienced by the two areas have led to the establishment of local ethnic minority communities, however the methods of data classification differ in each country and may be misleading; in Walsall 9.7% belong to 'Black', 'Asian', 'Chinese' or 'Other' ethnic groups (1991 Census) and in Mulhouse 16.9% are non-French nationals (1990 Census). The major difference which distinguishes the towns is their geographical location, Mulhouse situated close to the German and Swiss frontiers, Walsall at the heart of the English Midlands.

An appropriate research instrument, in the form of a written questionnaire, was developed. This quantitative method of data collection, which constituted the main substance of the research, involved the distribution of a total of almost 1000 questionnaires to pupils in 5 *collèges*, 2 *lycées professionnels* and 7 secondary schools on respective sides of the Channel. As the questionnaires were administered by the researcher, involving face to face contact, almost total success in completion was achieved. 330 of these questionnaires from each country have been processed to date and it is upon this sample of 660 that the results presented in this paper are based. The questionnaire comprised 56 questions, of which 6 are discussed here, devised to reveal pupil attitudes and perceptions about a variety of issues and areas believed to be connected with foreign language learning.

This paper will examine two areas – attitudes towards a changing Europe and anticipated use of the foreign language within future employment. Society's attitudes and values may be reflected in children by transmission through their parents and peers. The effect of, and conflict between, parental and peer group pressure in the formation of pupils' perceptions are captured through questions posed to the children. In-depth interviews, with an individually matched sample of 50 French/English pupils, extracted from the larger sample, allows further exploration of the quantitative data.

# Attitudes towards a changing Europe

The following graphs illustrate French and English pupil attitudes and perceptions in response to three questions concerning the EC. The quantitative data was coded and processed using Excel as a database. Weighted means (M) were calculated by using a 5 point ranking scale; 1 representing the most positive reaction and 5 the most negative. Value 3 could indicate a variety of reactions: 'I don't know', 'I don't care', 'I am uncertain' and will be referred to as the non-committal category.

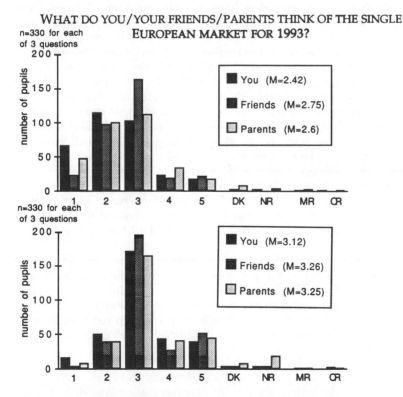

*Figure 1 French data (top) and Figure 2 English data (bottom)*
DK= don't know; NR= no response; MR=multiple response; OR= other response

The French and English data patterns, observed in response to the European question, differ greatly from one another. The skewed French pattern, reflected in the means, indicates a positive reaction on the whole from the French to a changing Europe and contrasts with the English attitudes. Simple inspection of the contrast between the means indicates a noteworthy level of significance.

The English graph however peaks at value 3, the non-committal category, the significance of which could be speculated as portraying an uninformed public, one which is unable to give an opinion, or perhaps one which is not interested. During the interviews the subject of Europe was raised by showing the pupils a picture of the European flag. Most Walsall children recognised the flag, but claimed never to have talked about nor heard their parents discussing European issues, which suggests that little discussion about Europe takes place within the home.

The general consensus of opinion on both sides of the Channel during interviewing was that friends' opinions about Europe were unknown as this was, hardly surprisingly, not a topic of hot debate and discussion in the school playground! This would account for the relatively high value 3 category for *friends* in both graphs. French pupils stated that Europe was discussed in geography classes as it was part of the official syllabus published by the Ministry of Education. It also transpired that many households in France watch and comment upon the *News* together as a family. As the data was collected during a period when the Maastricht referendum featured prominently in the media, there would have been no shortage of opportunity to discuss the changes taking place within the EC. Given that there was no referendum in Britain, coverage of this issue in the British media would certainly have differed in both nature and quantity. Another point to be borne in mind is that the Maastricht referendum result in Mulhouse was one of the most pro-European in the country, with 60.02% (l'Alsace, 21/9/92) voting 'oui', compared to 51.01 % (Le Monde, 22/9/92) in France as a whole.

The exposure or lack of exposure to European debate and the nature of discussion and analysis of European issues in the media, at home and at school contributes to the differences in attitude illustrated by these graphs. The other characteristic to be noted is the way the 3 different groups, *parents, peers* and *you*, move in step for both national groups. This endorses the idea that peers and parents do indeed influence the individual.

# Anticipated use of the foreign language within future employment

Responses to the three questions concerning future professional use of the foreign language can best be represented graphically as follows:

HOW USEFUL DO YOU/YOUR PARENTS/FRIENDS THINK THE FOREIGN
LANGUAGE WILL BE IN FUTURE EMPLOYMENT?

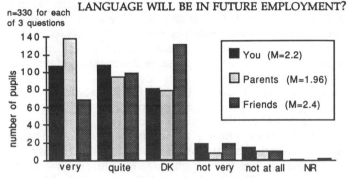

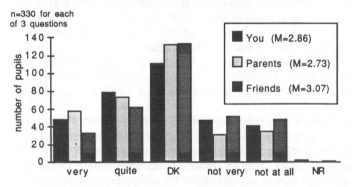

*Figure 3 above (French data) and Figure 4 below (English data)*

In response to the questions related to use of the FL in future employment, striking differences between the two sets of data can be observed, with the number of French responses indicating very useful more than doubling the English ones. The French data, illustrates clearly positive parental influence, reflected in the mean of 1.96. Parental encouragement was confirmed during interviews when pupils stressed the importance attached by their parents to education in general as well as to foreign language learning. This suggests that education in France is a high priority social value and that FLL is accorded high status by French society.

The English data is fairly evenly distributed, leaning slightly in the positive direction. However, the relatively high DK category suggests that little discussion and communication takes place both within the family and amongst peers on this subject. The DK category scores high in both sets of data for friends' opinions on usefulness of the FL in future employment, but whereas in the French data this appears to have little effect upon *you*, who remains firmly in line with parental opinion, the English data is grouped together for *parents, friends* and *you*. This, together with the high French response rate in the very useful category for both *parents* and *you*, indicates that parental pressure is the stronger influence at work in the French context. The relative importance of peer group and parental pressure is not clearly defined in the English data.

Such strong convictions on the part of the French pupils as to the importance of English for future professional use are somewhat surprising, given their geographical location, on the border with two German speaking countries. During an interview with one French school headmaster, he stated that it was his school's policy to advocate the learning of German rather than English, as the children would be far more likely to require German in later life. Only those children aiming to pursue higher education would benefit from English, he claimed, and that would be a small minority from his school. Official statistics reinforce the regional importance of German. In the Strasbourg *academie* 105,510 secondary pupils study German and 103,581 study English, which contrasts markedly with the national figures of 1,387,411 for German and 5,150,702 for English (Ministère de l'Education Nationale, 1992).

During interviews, the comparatively low importance accorded to French in future employment by the English, was further explored. Many pupils could place no or little future value on French. Some valued it extrinsically as another qualification with which to impress prospective employers, but no or little intrinsic value was mentioned. When questioned further as to possible situations which might call for foreign language skills, pupils cited traditional language jobs such as *translator* and *tourist guide, residence abroad* and most commonly *on holiday*. Evidence of high instrumental motivation is conspicuous by its absence in the English data drawn from these questions.

## Conclusions

The problem referred to in the opening paragraphs of this paper has been illustrated by the data presented, referring specifically to pupil perception of a changing Europe and anticipated use of the foreign language within a professional sphere. Some of the influences involved in attitude formation and the development of motivation in foreign language learning have been outlined. The transmission of attitudes and values through parents and peers to young adolescents is clearly illustrated by the parallel pattern of the graphs. Given that questions of an integrative nature have not been discussed within the confines of this paper, it has not been possible to pursue the relevance of the instrumental/integrative dichotomy which remains an avenue for future exploration.

However, from an instrumental viewpoint, with reference to FL use within future employment, contrasting perceived foreign language needs from both sides of the Channel have been illuminated. It would appear that French pupils perceive FLL to be of greater relevance to future employment than their English counterparts do. It would therefore appear from these initial results that this French sociolinguistic environment is more supportive of FLL than its English counterpart, in as much as it has succeeded in communicating to children the potential value of FLL with respect to future employment.

Until the criteria for securing employment within commerce and industry include FL skills, and such skills are consequently awarded high status by society at large, it is unlikely that we can expect an increase in instrumental FLL motivation in England. Concerning the European single market, in sharp contrast to the positive reception from French pupils, the English pupils sit firmly on the proverbial fence. Could the concept of a changing Europe and the envisaged future use of the FL be linked? Some of the children during the interviews in France certainly thought so.

# References

Burstall, C. (1970) *French in the Primary School – Attitudes and achievement.*
Hove, Sussex: King, Thorne and Stace Ltd.
Burstall, C. (1978). Factors affecting foreign language learning: a consideration of some recent research findings. In V. Kinsella, (ed.) *Language Teaching and Linguistics Surveys.* Cambridge: Cambridge University Press for CILT.
Byram, M. (1991) Reflections on otherness In *Times Educational Supplement*, 3/8/91
Department of Education and Science (1990) *Modern Foreign Languages for Ages 11-16* London: HMSO
Dörnyei, Z. (1990) Conceptualising motivation in foreign language learning. *Language Learning* 40, 1, 45-78.
Gardner, R.C. (1985) *Social Psychology and Second Language Learning: the role of attitude and motivation.* London: Edward Arnold.
Gardner, R.C. and Lambert, W.E. (1959) Motivation variables in second language acquisition. *Canadian Journal of Psychology* 13, 4.
Gardner, R.C. and MacIntyre, P.D. (1991) An instrumental motivation in language study. In *Studies in Second Language Acquisition*, 13, 1. Cambridge: Cambridge University Press.
Harmer, J. (1983) *The Practice of English Language Teaching.* London: Longman.

Lukmani, Yasmeen M. (1972) Motivation to learn and language proficiency. *Language Learning*, 22, 2, 261-73.

Ministère de l'Education Nationale (1985) *Collèges Programmes et Instructions* Paris: CNDP

Ministère de l'Education Nationale (1992) *Les Langues Vivantes dans le Second Degré en 1990-1991*. Note d'information 92.10.

O'Connell, B. (1973) Motivation, emotion and learning. In *Aspects of Learning*. Unwin Educational books.

Porcher, L. (1983) Appendix: reflections on language needs in the school. In R. Richterich (ed.) *Case studies in Identifying Needs*. Oxford: Pergamon Press.

Young, A.S. (1991) Unpublished M.A. thesis. University of Sheffield.